ASF

Atlantic views

D1330253

Advice to Readers

Every effort is made by our authors to ensure the accuracy of our guidebooks. However, changes can occur after a book has been printed. If you notice discrepancies between this guidebook and the facts on the ground, please let us know, either by email to enquiries@collinspress.ie or by post to The Collins Press, West Link Park, Doughcloyne, Wilton, Cork, T12 N5EF, Ireland.

To the memory of my brother Pádraig who gave me an appreciation for my life and those who dearly reside in it.

– DC

To individuals the world over who are prepared to go out and explore this amazing place we call home. Planet Earth.

– DE

Coastal views in Bunaw between Tousist and Lauragh.

CYCLING
KERRY
GREAT ROAD ROUTES

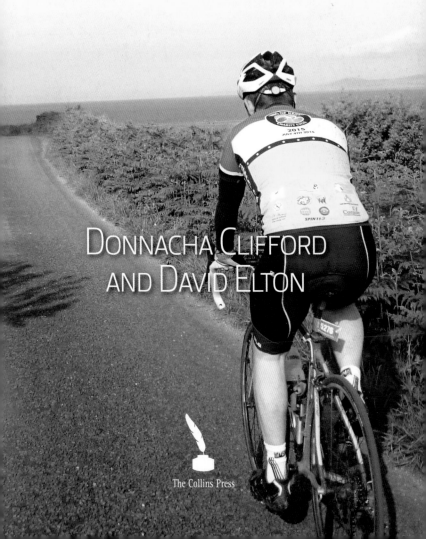

DONNACHA CLIFFORD
AND DAVID ELTON

The Collins Press

FIRST PUBLISHED IN 2017 BY
The Collins Press
West Link Park
Doughcloyne
Wilton
Cork
T12 N5EF
Ireland

Paperback ISBN: 978-1-84889-307-8
PDF eBook ISBN: 978-1-84889-602-4
EPUB eBook ISBN: 978-1-84889-603-1
Kindle ISBN: 978-1-84889-604-8

Design and typesetting by Fairways Design
Typeset in Myriad Pro
Printed in Poland by Białostockie Zakłady Graficzne SA

Contents

Routes

Acknowledgements

For giving us great support, we would like to thank our friends in the Currow Cycling Club and the Chain Gang Cycling Club in Tralee, who nurtured our love of cycling and who first guided us on the roads of Kerry, which we did not yet know, and who gave us a sense of adventure to continue that exploration even further.

To our friends and families, without whose love and support this book would not have been possible. With special mention reserved for Liz Elton and Ciara Tangney for their patience and understanding.

To our proof-readers who provided valuable feedback on our work and who sanity-checked both us and our words: Fiona Cooke, Aileen Clifford, Carmel Kelly, Donal Browne, Lorna Browne, Tomas Crowley, Maeve Higgins, John Murray, Aine Horan, Denis Clifford, Helen Blanchfield, Padraig Heaphy and Mike O'Connell.

To our publisher, The Collins Press, for supporting us along the way, putting us at ease when we needed direction.

We would also like to thank everyone we bounced ideas off during the year, whose names are too many to mention.

Map of Route Start Points

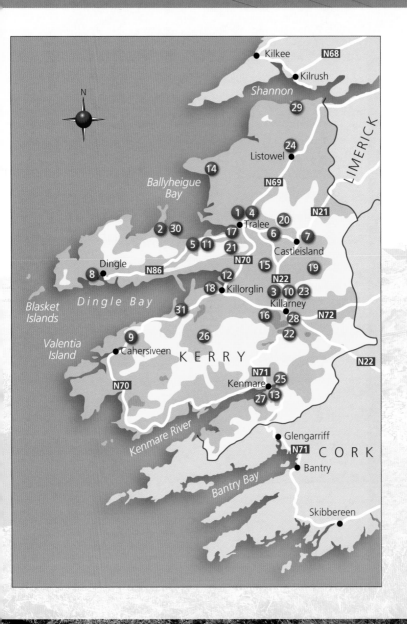

Quick-Reference Route Table

No.	Route	Starting Point	Grade
1	The Casement Tour	Tralee	1/2
2	Brandon Point-to-Point	Castlegregory	2/3
3	Ballyhar & Milltown Loop	Killarney	2/3
4	Kerry Head	Tralee	2
5	Camp and Maharees Loop	Camp	2/3
6	The Butter Road	Maglass	3
7	The Three Counties Cycle	Castleisland	3/4
8	Slea Head	Dingle	3
9	Valentia Island and The Skellig Ring	Cahersiveen	3/4
10	The Ring of Killarney	Killarney	3/4
11	Annascaul, Minard and Bothar na gCloch	Camp	3/4
12	King Puck Route	Milltown	3
13	Priest's Leap and The Borlin Valley	Kenmare	4/5
14	North Kerry Hurling Tour	Ballyheigue	2/3
15	Killarney to Tralee: the Hidden Roads	Firies	3
16	The Gap of Dunloe and The Black Valley	Killarney	4
17	The Lacey Cup Circuit	Tralee	3/4
18	Cromane, Rossbeigh and Caragh Lake	Killorglin	3/4
19	Sliabh Luachra Loop	Rathmore	4
20	The Dan Paddy Andy Figure of Eight	Maglass	4
21	The Conor Pass Circuit	Blennerville	5
22	Sneem and Kenmare Loop	Torc	4
23	The Three Climbs and Two Counties Cycle	Killarney	4
24	North Kerry and the Coast Road	Listowel	4
25	Kenmare and Coom	Kenmare	4/5
26	Mini Ring of Kerry	Glencar	5
27	The Ring of Beara	Kenmare	5
28	The Ring of Kerry	Killarney	5
29	Wild Atlantic Way 1	Tarbert	4
30	Wild Atlantic Way 2	Castlegregory	4/5
31	Wild Atlantic Way 3	Glenbeigh	5

Range	Distance (km)	Ascent (m)	Time	Page
Short	38	230	1½–2 hours	16
Short	44	452	2–2½ hours	20
Short	45	361	2–2½ hours	24
Short	48	306	2–3 hours	28
Short	48	328	2–2½ hours	32
Mid	52	542	2½–3 hours	36
Mid	53	652	2½–3 hours	40
Mid	54	603	1½–2½ hours	44
Mid	56	733	2½–3 hours	48
Mid	59	607	2–2½ hours	53
Mid	62	915	2½–3½ hours	57
Mid	62	428	3–4 hours	62
Mid	65	1,050	3½–4 hours	66
Mid	68	388	3–3½ hours	70
Mid	68	739	3–4 hours	74
Mid	73	1,076	3½–4 hours	78
Mid	74	662	3–3½ hours	83
Mid	74	756	3–3½ hours	87
Mid	80	885	3½–4 hours	91
Mid	83	950	3½–4 hours	95
Long	89	1,201	4–5 hours	99
Mid	90	1,243	4–4½ hours	103
Long	100	1,201	4–4½ hours	107
Long	100	870	4½–5 hours	111
Long	100	1,344	4½–5½ hours	115
Long	104	1,358	4½–5½ hours	120
Long	140	1,485	6–7 hours	124
Long	170	1,741	7½–9 hours	128
Long	126	842	6–7 hours	134
Long	148	1,548	6½–7½ hours	139
Long	161	1,932	7–8 hours	145

Introduction

With the popularity of cycling steadily increasing in Ireland over the past few years, it seems that everyone and their mother are now out on their bikes. In Kerry the cycling scene has kept a pace with the national trend and this has largely been supported by the National Bike-to-Work Scheme as well as the running of probably one of the most popular cycling events in the country, the Ring of Kerry cycle. This annual charity event is run on the first Saturday of July and sees many cyclists training on Kerry roads from early on in the year, in preparation for the event. The Wild Atlantic Way has also been a very popular campaign to get visitors into the region and what better way to explore Kerry's more than 400km of rugged and beautiful coastline than by bicycle?

The aim of this guidebook is to detail some of the most popular cycling routes in the county but also to encourage cyclists to travel some roads that are perhaps less well known. With over 2,500km of cycling terrain covered in this guide we are confident that there are routes to suit all cycling abilities, from the very casual cyclist to the very experienced.

As you would expect in a county with many mountain regions there are many climbs encountered in this book as part of our routes. Each climb has its own personality and is difficult to judge without experiencing in person. Most are manageable with a moderate amount of fitness and adequate gearing. Most cyclists that we know enjoy a challenge or two and they should certainly be satisfied by what the roads of County Kerry have to offer.

Happy cycling!

Route 20: Knocknagoshel, heading west towards Dan Paddy Andy cross and Tralee.

Using this book

Grading

The grading of each route in this book is based on distance and level of difficulty from 1 to 5 and is categorised as follows:

1. A relatively short cycle with gentle or short climbs.
2. Short/middle-distance cycles with relatively easy climbing efforts.
3. Middle-distance cycles with easy/moderate climbs included.
4. Middle/longer-distance cycles with some challenging climbs included.
5. Typically longer-distance cycles with tough climbs.

Generally speaking, the shorter a cycle, the easier it will be; however, keep a close eye on the vertical metres gained, and the elevation chart which is a good guide as to whether or not there are some tough climbs in a particular route. For example, the King Puck route is 62km in length with 428m of climbing while the Valentia Island and Skellig Ring route is 56km in length with 733 metres of climbing involved, with the latter route being considerably more difficult that the former, even though the King Puck route is longer.

We have calculated the route times based on an average speed of 23km/h. These times do not include stops for any kind of break as these can vary from person to person.

Gradients and statistics for the routes in this guide were sourced from MapMyRide.com and Strava.com, which allowed us to analyse data from routes that we had cycled using GPS devices.

The route maps are provided with a map scale that can differ from map to map and each map also has a compass and directional arrows for orientation. Be sure to familiarise yourself with the map, directions and place names that will be travelled throughout your planned cycle. In the odd case where signposting is lacking we have tried our best to describe the directions of the cycle but for the majority of our routes we have found signs and directions to be adequate. If in doubt, a quick check on your position with the help of a mobile phone is useful. Failing that we have always found locals and passers-by to be friendly and more than helpful with directions.

Equipment

The cycles in this guide are best experienced on a racer or hybrid bike that is relatively light and sturdy. This is important especially for the middle- or longer-distance cycles. Mountain bikes are heavier and, although arguably more comfortable, can make travelling on road seem like a slog at times.

It is worthwhile trying to be as self-sufficient on the bike as possible. This means being able to fix a puncture and making sure that your bike is in roadworthy condition. At a minimum, carry a portable/mini pump and a number of spare tubes and be comfortable with having to change a puncture as, unfortunately, they will happen.

With regards to being seen, high-visibility clothing and cycle lighting make it easier for motorists and other road users to see you and so are very important.

No cycle should be undertaken without a helmet.

Cycle clothing is easily available nowadays and the clothing needs of each cycle will differ for many reasons. Comfortable shorts and gloves and shoes are important as they cover the three touch points with the bike. Cycling glasses can keep flies away from your eyes and prevent you from having a weepy moment on fast descents, and are also useful in helping to maintain visibility on sunny days.

Safety

As already stated a roadworthy bike, a helmet and high-visibility clothing are all essential for your safety. Here is some other important advice:

- Be sure to cycle on the left of the road and as close to the road margin as is safely possible. Sometimes, debris, potholes or obstacles might prevent you from staying close to the road margin; be sure to look over your shoulder and ensure that no traffic is coming before signalling and moving out slightly to avoid them.
- Always try to be aware of your environment: listen for oncoming traffic from behind and ahead of you. To that end we don't recommend cycling with headphones.
- Before turning left or right, always let your intention be known to other road users by indicating with your arms.
- There had been a recent surge in bike theft. If leaving bikes unattended for a time at coffee stops, either securely lock the bikes, put them in a safe and visible place, or agree on a rota with a companion to mind the bikes.
- On a practical note, some of the routes in this guide travel through remote mountainous areas which can be devoid of a good mobile signal in parts. Ensure to tell someone about your route plans before you head out if travelling alone.

Climate

Ireland's temperate climate and prevailing south-westerly winds mean unpredictable weather. Our warmest months are also our wettest. County Kerry seems at times to get the brunt of the Atlantic wind and rain. With a little preparation and proper clothing, however, it is still possible to enjoy cycling in Kerry most of the year round. Keep a close eye on the weather forecast and bring adequate clothing. An easily folded rain cape is always a good option, just in case. How many layers of clothing you should wear depends on personal preference but warm clothing can be your best friend for many cycles in spring, autumn and winter.

Contacts

Emergency Services: For all emergencies dial 999. This includes the Garda Síochána, ambulance, fire brigade, mountain rescue and coastguard. You can also dial the EU number 112, which connects to the same services. Both numbers are free of charge.

Weather Forecast: For weather forecasts check the Met Éireann website (www.met.ie) or www.mountain-forecast.com. The accuweather.com app also has good information.

Map Information

Map information from this book was based on GPS and maps generated using MapMyRide.com and Strava.com.

Websites

There are over 400 cycling clubs and 26,000 members in Ireland affiliated with Cycling Ireland: www.cyclingireland.ie

Our website, www.KerryCycling.com, has some useful information for cycling in County Kerry, including details on cycling clubs and routes.

Other useful and interesting websites are:

www.boards.ie/cycling
www.irishcycling.com
https://www.google.ie/maps
www.stickybottle.com
www.strava.com
http://www.wildatlanticway.com/
www.womenscycling.ie

1. The Casement Tour

Tralee – Ardfert – Banna – Barrow – Churchill – Fenit – The Kerries – Tralee

A historical pocket of north Kerry.

Grade:	1/2
Distance:	38km
Height gain:	230m
Time:	1½ to 2 hours
Climbs:	No major climbs on this route

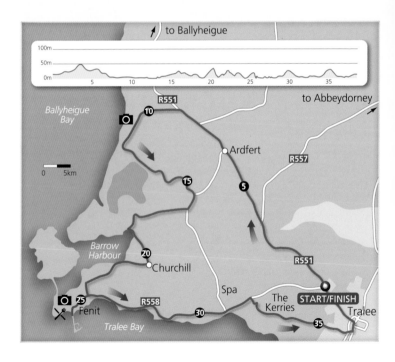

Start/finish

The starting point for this route is from the Mounthawk area of Tralee. From the centre of Tralee follow the **R551** in the direction of Ballyheigue and Fenit. Within 2km, there are parking facilities located just to the right of Mounthawk Roundabout.

Entering Ardfert village with Glandore Gate to the right.

I n 2016, Ireland celebrated the centenary of the Easter Rising in Dublin and the nation's eventual independence. A precursor to the uprising occurred in these parts of north Kerry: Sir Roger Casement landed from a German submarine, U-19, on 'lonely Banna Strand', and was arrested nearby, following a failed attempt to land a consignment of arms in Tralee Bay for the Easter Rising.

This route captures a little of that modern history as well as the ancient history of Ardfert village, its surrounding areas and the local spiritual leader, St Brendan the Navigator, a fifth-century monk who is said to have discovered the New World and sailed to North America long before the Vikings or Christopher Columbus.

Route description

At the roundabout follow the **R551** north in the direction of Ardfert and Ballyheigue. The first section of road between Tralee and Ardfert is a mere 8km and is generally flat, except for one small hill beyond Ballyroe Hotel. On entering Ardfert, a small detour is optional, to visit the twelfth-century Ardfert Cathedral and the nearby Ardfert Abbey. These buildings are dedicated to St Brendan, who was born in the vicinity in AD 484.

The countryside between Barrow and Churchill.

Continuing on towards Ballyheigue, take the first left towards Banna Strand, heading westwards. You can continue to the strand itself and take in some of the fresh Atlantic air, but our route takes a left turn, at the crossroads, just beyond Sir Roger's campsite. Within 1km, the monument for Sir Roger Casement comes into view. It was here that Casement and his two companions rested after coming ashore from the German submarine U-19 after it had failed to rendezvous with the German cargo ship *Aud* in 1916, which was due to land a consignment of arms nearby. This attempt to land arms in Kerry was to assist the imminent rising in Dublin.

From the monument, take a right at the fork in the road; follow the twisting route through the sand dunes before the road straightens out and moves away from the coast, travelling over tidal salt marshes at Carrahane.

It was close to this section of the route that the unfortunate Casement sought refuge as he struggled on, weak and with a high fever. About a kilometre on, the tree-lined area of McKenna's Fort, an ancient 'Fairy Fort' or ring fort, can be seen on the left, just off the road. It was in this area that Casement was hiding when he was arrested by the RIC police.

Taking the next right turn (made distinctive by a black pole with a yellow walker sign), proceed along the narrow road. Turn right at the T-junction, and then take the second right, signposted for Tralee Golf Club. Along this stretch of road there are fine panoramic views of the Slieve Mish Mountains, stretching from Castlemaine in the east to Dingle and beyond to the west.

The road then sweeps down towards Barrow Harbour. Take a left at the T-junction. (Right will lead to the popular Tralee Golf Club, designed by Arnold Palmer.) Follow the road over the causeway and humpback bridge and up the hill to Churchill. Just before the church and graveyard, take the right turn, signposted for Fenit, and enjoy a nice fast descent towards the hamlet of Chapeltown along the south side of Barrow Harbour and on towards the townland of Tawlaght in the direction of Fenit. Turn right at the T-junction, just beyond the Old Lighthouse Hotel, into Fenit village. In Fenit there are various options to refuel. There is a public toilet close to the beach, located opposite the Tralee Bay Sailing Club and Sailing School. For something a little different, it is possible to cycle partly up the pier (be careful of the old railway tracks) and explore Samphire Island and the statue of St Brendan, or just relax close to the small beach overlooking the lighthouse on Little Samphire Rock and reflect on a job well done. On a clear day the mountain ranges on the Dingle Peninsula are clearly visible from here. Mike's cafe and the Westend Bar are nearby.

On leaving Fenit, most of the route back to Tralee is accompanied by Tralee Bay, which sits peacefully to the right. The route passes quickly through Kilfenora and up the hill to The Spa. After leaving The Spa village, take the first road to the right, after the cricket pitch (it is not signposted!). This lovely narrow but rolling road leads back into Tralee via the Kerries area of the town. From here on continue through farmland and past eye-catching properties, before rolling down into the more densely populated Spa Road. On reaching the T-junction at Kerins O'Rahillys GAA club, take a left turn past the Bon Secours Hospital and on to a mini-roundabout. Take the first exit off the roundabout, following signs for Ardfert and Fenit onto the **R874**. Continue straight ahead until the traffic lights. Take a left turn onto the **R551**. Your starting point is less than 2km away.

The descent from Churchill, heading towards Fenit.

2. Brandon Point to Point

Castlegregory – Ballyhoneen – Cloghane – Brandon Point – Brandon – Stradbally – Castlegregory

Rugged coastlines and stunning ocean views in west Kerry.

Grade: 2/3	**Height gain:** 452m	
Distance: 44km	**Time:** 2 to 2½ hours	
Climb:		

Category	Length	Start/End Points	Start/End Elevation	Average Gradient
4	2.3km	20.56km / 23.0km	9m / 92m	4%

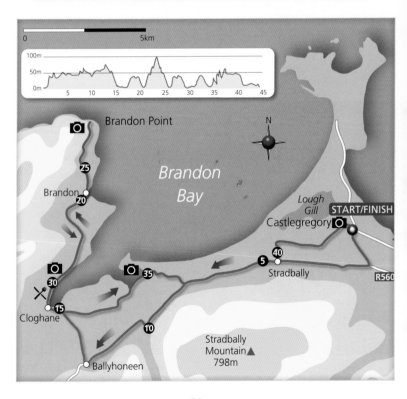

The road to Cloghane.

Start/finish

This route starts in the west Kerry village of Castlegregory, about 26km west of Tralee on the Dingle Peninsula. There is limited parking in the Tailor's Row area of the village.

Most people visting the Dingle Peninsula will first head to the town of Dingle and then further west out towards the scenic Slea Head, leaving the pocket of land to the north-east of Mount Brandon that little bit quieter. The villages of Cloghane and Brandon are often the starting point for walkers and hikers making the trek up Mount Brandon or exploring many of the stunning walking routes in the area. Water-sports enthusiasts take advantage of the spectacular sea and surf conditions here. From a cycling perspective the area is often overlooked in favour of the nearby Conor Pass. This cycle route takes the two-wheeled adventurer along the rugged ocean coastline of this secluded north-western section of this peninsula. One can view the deserted sandy beaches, cycle the quiet country roads adorned by colourful wild fauna and take in the picturesque villages of Cloghane and Brandon.

Route description

Taking a left turn out of the car park, proceed up Tailor's Row and out of Castlgregory onto the **R560**. At the junction with the main road, turn right in the direction of Dingle and the Conor Pass. At this early stage the route

Alongside the water's edge at Fermoyle.

has already gained a few metres in height and there are fine views down towards the strands at Kilcummin and Fermoyle, with Mount Brandon and Brandon Point visible to the west. The road then moves quickly inland towards the Conor Pass ascent. Although this route doesn't actually take in any of the pass it comes mightily close. At the foot of the pass take the right turn at Kilmore Cross, Ballyhoneen for Cloghnane (An Clochán); this is now the Gaeltacht (Irish-speaking) area. Proceed down a smooth, speedy descent with forestry on either side. At the junction, turn left and cycle into Cloghane. As the route passes through the village it pursues a coastal inlet to the east, offering glimpses of the adjacent beaches and the Slieve Mish Mountains in the distance. Between this point and the next village, Brandon, the road, although in very good condition, takes on more of a rolling nature with one or two testing hills.

On entering Brandon, a short but worthwhile detour would be to cycle off to the right and view the pier, which offers uninterrupted views out across Brandon Bay towards Castlegregory, the Maharees and north Kerry. There is also a small beach in the vicinity. Once beyond Brandon, the climb towards the point begins. From a climbing perspective it is a steady 2.3km ascent with an average gradient of 4%. The road narrows quite considerably, with just enough space to squeeze past any oncoming vehicles. The road surface, although not up to the previous quality, is acceptable enough, with just the odd broken area. At the summit the area levels out and opens up into a much wider space, which is used as a car park, viewing point and the start of a coastal hiking trail. As might be expected, the views out to the north and east are stunning, provided the weather is agreeable.

The descent back into Brandon is routine enough with the only danger being one or two blind bends where there might be a car, a bike or hikers coming in the opposite direction. For a coffee break, Brandon or Cloghane are ideal spots, with a handful of pubs and an excellent bakery opposite the church in Cloghane keen to offer a friendly welcome.

Having cycled through Cloghane, keep to the left following the Castlegregory and Tralee signposts. This section of the cycle keeps the coast on the left as the route sweeps across two rivers and runs adjacent to a small natural harbour at Fermoyle. Continue up the slight incline, meeting up once again with the **R560**. Turn left and continue on in an easterly direction. On entering Stradbally take a left turn, signposted for Castlegregory Golf Course and Stradbally Strand. Follow the slight descent north before taking the first right turn before an old stone bridge. The landscape is now very flat and agricultural, with high hedgerows on either side of the road, protecting the traveller from the occasional Atlantic gust. Over to the left there are glimpses of Lough Gill, lying inconspicuously amongst the patchwork of fields and distant sand dunes. This road will bring you back into Castlegregory, where you proceed straight along Strand Street before taking a right turn at Fitzgerald's Bar into Post Office Square. The starting point lies a little more than 200m to the left.

Climbing away from Fermoyle.

3. Ballyhar and Milltown Loop

Killarney – Ballyhar – Milltown – Aghadoe Heights – Killarney

A short but challenging route on peaceful laneways.

Grade: 2/3			**Height gain:** 361m		
Distance: 45km			**Time:** 2 to 2½ hours		
Climbs:					
Category	Length	Start/End Points	Start/End Elevation	Average Gradient	
5	2.5km	15km / 17.5km	38m / 107m	2.8%	
5	2.8km	40km / 42.8km	59m / 109m	1.8%	

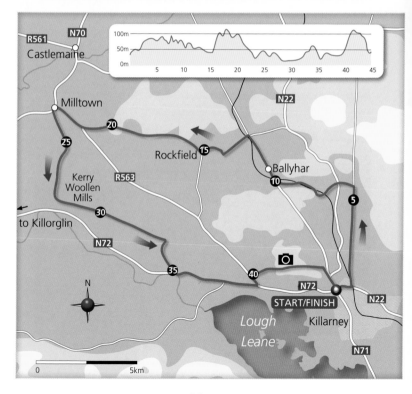

Start/Finish

The Cleeney Roundabout is located to the west of Killarney, where the **N72** and **N22** meet. There should be limited cark parking spaces close by with good access from all directions.

Milltown.

Mid Kerry is the area that many tourists cross to reach the county's more publicised destinations, but in slowing the pace down on a bicycle and taking time to explore these little-known back roads, the hidden beauty of the countryside begins to reveal itself, offering laneways where the sound of nature takes precedence over that of the motorcar, with plenty of viewing points to pause and glimpse the eye-catching views of the better-known landmarks, such as the MacGillycuddy's Reeks, Carrantuohill, the Lakes of Killarney and the Dingle Peninsula.

Route description

From Cleeney Roundabout take the **N22** in the direction of Cork. After almost 1km, take a left turn onto the Kilcummin road. Initially the road follows the railway line before rising up quite steeply with a challenging 'S' bend, before a crossroads. Proceed straight across in a northerly direction, following a moderately flat road until reaching a crossroads called Finnegan's Cross. From here, turn left onto the **L3009**. On reaching the crossroads at the **N22**, proceed straight across and onto the **L3004.**

This stretch of road cuts through a rugged forested landscape, crossing the railway line and in certain parts becoming quite narrow. After about

On the way up to Aghadoe.

3km on this stretch turn right at the T-junction, onto the **L2019**. Proceed once more over the Tralee-to-Dublin railway line before cycling up a moderately steep hill to Ballyhar. Follow this stretch of road for the next 2.5km before taking a left turn onto the **L3023**, signposted for Milltown.

Over the next 2.7km, the road traverses another railway crossing at one point and is protected mainly by tall hedgerows and trees. The route soon reaches a crossroads with a metal workshop to the right. Take the road up to the right signed for Rockfield Stud Farm. Here, the road climbs sharply. After less than 200m, take the next left. This is an unmarked road, looking rather like a track, with tufts of grass growing in its centre. From here on, the steep ascent continues. The good news is that the road improves slightly and widens before eventually levelling out. Once at the summit, enjoy the spectacular views of the MacGillycuddy's Reeks to the left, and the Slieve Mish mountains and Dingle Peninsula straight ahead. Continuing on for another 2km take a right turn close to Rockfield School. Within 5km, this section of road will eventually lead onto the **R563**.

At the junction, take a right turn and proceed down the hill into Milltown. Although a small village, Milltown is a good place for refreshments, with shops and a bakery. Milltown hosted the world bodhrán championships from 2006 to 2011.

On reaching the bottom of the hill and the centre of the village, bear left onto the **N70** towards Killorglin. Follow the bend in the road and the climb out of the village. Take the left turn onto the road signed Lyre/ Recycling Centre. This section of road is relatively flat and runs through a rural and rugged landscape, with scattered woodland, hedgerows and small bungalows. After 4.4km from Milltown, take the left turn at the second crossroads, heading east. The road is unmarked, but known locally as Kerry Woollen Mills.

The terrain is similar to the previous stretch of road but with more of an agricultural feel to the area. Continue eastwards as the straight road now becomes Lahard Cottages road. At this point the road narrows slightly and the surface becomes a little uneven. The route reaches a T-junction at Faha Glen. Turn right and continue on as the road descends steadily towards the **N72** Ring of Kerry route.

At the **N72** turn left and head east towards Killarney. Within 4km of cycling on what can be a busy stretch of road, take the left turn onto the **R563**, at the Golden Nugget pub. Within 500m, take a right turn, signed for Aghadoe. Follow the road up the gentle incline and past the church on the right. The road starts to take a few twists and turns, before becoming steeper. This climb is less than 2km, but is steep in parts. At the summit, you will find the Aghadoe Heights Hotel on the left. To the right is a viewing area that is well worth a visit. From here there are great views of the Killarney lakes and beyond. There is also a handy panoramic map identifying all the landmarks.

Continue to the T-junction for the **L2019**. Turn right and go down the steep descent. On reaching the **N22** take the right turn and continue down the short descent into Killarney and to the finishing point.

Decisions. We go left to Milltown.

4. Kerry Head

Tralee – Ardfert – Ballyheigue – Kerry Head – Ballyheigue
– Ardfert – Tralee

An invigorating circuit with stunning views of the Atlantic
Ocean and north Kerry coastline as well as the Dingle
Peninsula and County Clare on a good day.

Grade: 2

Distance: 48km

Climb:

Height gain: 306m

Time: 2 to 3 hours

Category	Length	Start/End Points	Start/End Elevation	Average Gradient
4	5km	14km / 23km	27m / 152m	3%

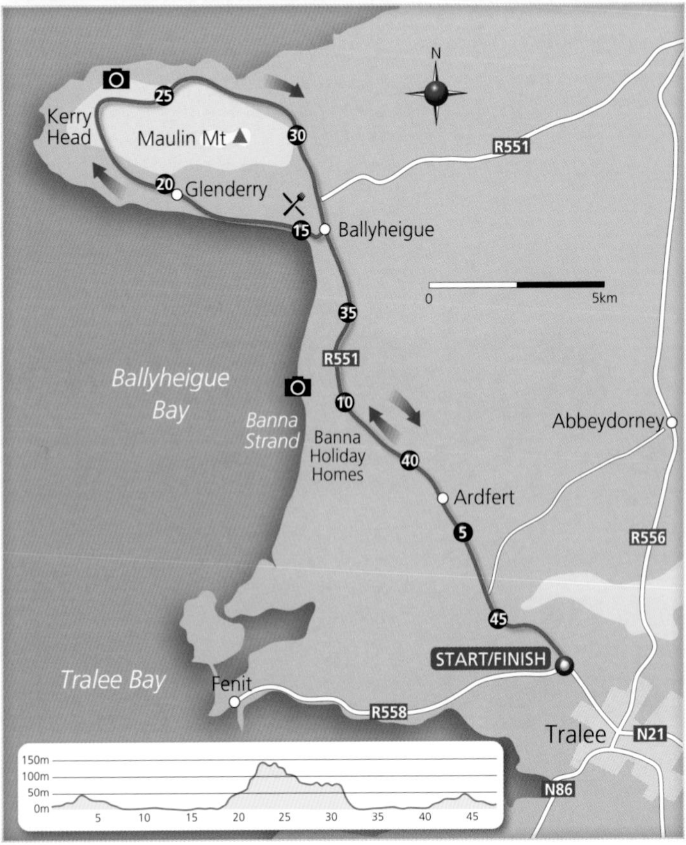

Views of Mount Brandon and Dingle Peninsula from Kerry Head.

Start/Finish

This is a very accessible route and can be started from any location within Tralee. For the easiest access, we recommend starting at Mounthawk Roundabout, which is at the junction of the **R551, R558** and **Bracker O'Regan** roads on the north side of the town where there is parking and immediate access to the **R551**.

Kerry Head is a headland in the north-west of the county and offers a beautiful loop with sea views, quiet roads and the very best of fresh air! This route approaches Kerry Head from the direction of Tralee, passing through the picturesque village of Ardfert and close to historic Banna Strand, before reaching Ballyheigue, the gateway to Kerry Head, where timeless views of the Atlantic coastline appear before you and where the highlight of your journey begins.

Route description

From Tralee begin your journey northwards, following signposts for Ardfert and Ballyheigue along the **R551**. The first 8km of the route as far as Ardfert is quite rolling with a short and gentle ascent from Ballyroe and a welcome descent practically all the way into Ardfert. At Ardfert there is a crossroads: be sure to continue through the village along the **R551**, signposted for Ballyheigue. Take a moment in Ardfert to enjoy the ruins of Ardfert Cathedral. Built in 1117 and dedicated to St Brendan, it still dominates the landscape for miles around.

The view towards Ballybunion at the top of the Kerry Head climb.

Over the next 8km the coastal landscape gradually begins to open up as the route passes a signpost to the left for Banna Strand, which is an optional detour on this route and approximately an additional 3.8km round trip to the beach from the main road and back again. The beach is not only famous for its natural amenities but also for being the spot where Roger Casement and others landed on 21 April 1916 when trying to land arms for the Irish republicans and the imminent Easter Rising.

After approximately 16km you will reach the coastal village of Ballyheigue. Take a left turn following a signpost for Kerry Head, entering the heart of the village. Ballyheigue has a selection of small shops and a café or two and is a good place for a quick stop if you need to refuel or simply take a breather and enjoy the views that Ballyheigue beach offers.

As you leave Ballyheigue village, the Kerry Head loop can be said to start for real. This section of the route will take you along the headland on narrower but mostly well-surfaced roads. On leaving the village you will notice that the gradient increases as you begin to climb the 5km category 4 climb with an average gradient of 3%. As climbs go, it is pretty gentle with a slight sting towards the tail end and a bit of respite in the middle as it levels off for a short while. To your left all the way along this climb some of the spectacular views become apparent with the Dingle Peninsula and Brandon Mountain to your left and Banna Strand and Ballyheigue behind you. You will know you are at the top of the climb after approximately 24km, when you can see further views of the sea stacks at Ballybunion to the north-east and Loop Head in County Clare to the north. This is a good point to stop and take in all that the scenery has to offer.

Continue on along the headland now where you will descend at pace back towards Ballyheigue. If you are in the mood for exploring at approximately the 28km mark there is a signpost to the left for a short return detour to Tobar Daitleann, a holy well and clear spring believed to have healing properties. Continue along the main headland road following signposts for Ballyheigue and you will come to a T-junction marked left for Causeway and right for Ballyheigue. Take the right-hand option and on entering Ballyheigue you will have approximately 33km completed. From here travel back along your initial route, following the **R551** towards Ardfert, arriving back in Tralee, having completed 48km.

Tobar Daithleann, a holy well on the Kerry Head Loop.

5. Camp and Maharees Loop

Camp – Gleann na nGealt – Castlegregory – Maharees – Stradbally – Kilgobbin – Camp

Ancient folklore with a breath of sea air, in the concealed laneways of west Kerry.

Grade: 2/3

Distance: 48km

Climb:

Height gain: 328m

Time: 2 to 2½ hours

Category	Length	Start/End Points	Start/End Elevation	Average Gradient
5	3km	0.6km / 3.6km	41m / 150m	3.6%

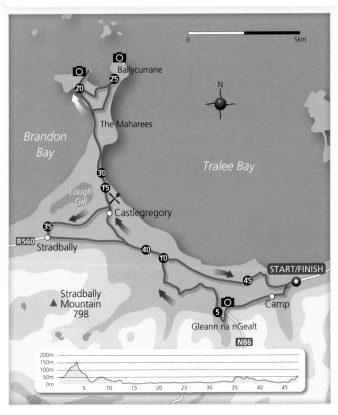

Start/Finish

The starting point for this route is located in Lower Camp, opposite the Railway Tavern Bar on the **N86** road. There is ample parking just to the side of the main road. Camp village is approximately 16km west of Tralee.

The area of west Kerry and the Dingle Peninsula are famed more for Dingle town and the neighbouring Slea Head. However, like much of Kerry, the west holds many hidden gems, provided you are prepared to dig a little.

This route navigates varied landscapes, from the breathtaking descent into Gleann na nGealt to the European Low Countries-style flats on the approach to Castlegregory. The route then stretches out to the north, exploring the Maharees, with its sandy laneways, golden sands and clear waters that are so popular with water-sports enthusiasts in the warmer months, set against the backdrop of Mount Brandon and its neighbouring peaks.

Route description

Follow the **N86** to the west, towards Dingle. Take a left turn for Annascaul, continuing on the **N86** through Camp (upper) village. Beyond the village the vista opens up to reveal stunning views of the Atlantic Ocean and Mount Brandon. The climb from Camp is approximately 1km before the route takes a right turn, signposted for Foilatrisnig. From here the road has a surprisingly good surface, descending into Gleann na nGealt. The area has a hint of the lower Alps, with streams, wild flowers and trees prevalent along the roadside.

The slip road off the N86 2km west of Camp village, heading down to Gleann na nGealt, with Stradbally Mountain ahead.

Once in the Gleann na nGealt ('Valley of the Mad'), the route twists back in a northerly direction along a steady descent. When in the valley, keep an eye out for the ancient well on the left-hand side of the road. Legend has it that the waters have healing properties for madness; tests in 2012 found higher-than-normal traces of lithium in the water, proving there is an element of truth in this local legend. On reaching the T-junction, take the left turn (unmarked). Within 500m take a second left (also unmarked) and follow the road around through old farmsteads to another T-junction. Here you will see a derelict cottage on the left of the junction. Take the right-hand turn and continue towards the main **R560**.

At the **R560** take a left turn towards Castlegregory. The cycle on this stretch of road is for no more than 800m, before taking a second right (signed Kerry Cottages holiday homes). Continue down a smooth descent with the Atlantic Ocean in full view ahead, before taking a left-hand turn and cycling onto part of the famous Dingle Way walking route. The landscape here is quite similar to Holland and the Low Countries: flat, sandy and tree-less, with dykes and drainage on either side of the road. A glimpse up to the left is a good reminder that you are still in Kerry, though, as the mountains sweep majestically down towards the coast. On entering Castlegregory, turn right onto Tailors Row and proceed through the village to a crossroads. Go straight across. Follow the signs for Kilsha and Fahamore. This is the road onto the Maharees.

The Maharees is a peninsula 6km long and 500m wide. It comes to life in the summer with a number of campsites and surfing attractions. The road here remains flat as it cuts through the sand dunes. This can leave the road coated at times in sand, which is not always the best of surfaces for a bike! The route eventually leads to a pub, Spillane's Bar. At this

Fahamore Harbour, Maharees.

Taking a pause in Kilgobbin, Camp.

point the route temporally hugs the seafront, before leading to Fahamore Harbour, a pier frequented by fishing boats, anglers and divers. Take time to appreciate the spectacular views of Fenit and north Kerry to the east.

Retrace the road back to Spillane's Bar and after approximately 500m take the road to the left, signposted The Green Rooms bar, O'Connors. Follow the road as it takes a slight right turn. Once more the ocean comes into view and accompanies the route as it reaches the area of Ballycurrane and the furthest point north on the peninsula. The old graveyard just up to the left is well worth a quick visit. Many of the graves are decorated with brightly coloured hand-painted designs.

Retrace the road back to Castlegregory, which is approximately 6km. On reaching Castlegregory, there is time for a quick coffee and snack before taking a right-hand turn away from the village onto Strand Street towards Dingle and the west. The route leads towards Castlegregory golf course and follows a flat, winding road for approximately 1km; take the left turn just before an old stone bridge, following the slight incline towards Stradbally. Once in the village take a left turn onto the **R560**, heading in the direction of Camp and Tralee.

From here the route becomes wider and slightly busier with traffic. Proceed eastwards, passing the Seven Hogs Bar; after 3.5km from the Seven Hogs, take the left turn signposted Beach and Shore Acre Caravan Park. Continue along the narrow road into the hamlet of Kilgobbin, which is dominated by an eye-catching Norman church. If you wish, take a 50m detour to the beach, down to the left of the church. Keeping the church to the left, follow the road around as it twists its way up a slight incline and back to rejoin the **R560**. Turn left towards Tralee. Within 1km of here the route comes to its conclusion, with the start/finish point just on the right.

6. The Butter Road

Maglass – Castleisland – Cordal – Butter Road – Scartaglen
– Currow – Currans – Gortatlea – Maglass

Some interesting early climbing on the quiet back roads of east Kerry.

Grade: 3			**Height gain:** 542m		
Distance: 52km			**Time:** 2½ to 3 hours		
Climb:					

Category	Length	Start/End Points	Start/End Elevation	Average Gradient
2	7.7km	12km / 19.7km	97m / 322m	3.3%

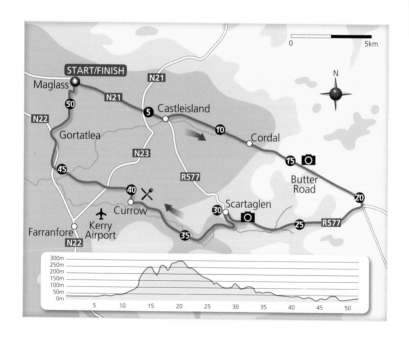

A panoramic view of east Kerry on the Butter Road close to the R577 junction.

Start/Finish

From Tralee, take the **N21** in the direction of Castleisland and Limerick. The starting point is at O'Riada's Bar at Maglass in Ballymacelligott, which is clearly visible from the main road at the midway point between Tralee and Castleisland. There is ample parking close to the bar.

The Butter Road was an eighteenth-century road from Castleisland which ran in an almost straight line to the Butter Exchange in Cork city. This route travels a small but hilly section of the Butter Road, before doubling back along the lush Brown Flesk River valley and through the serene villages of Scartaglen, Currow and Currans.

Route description

From the starting point, take a left turn and travel east along the **N21** towards Castleisland. Take the second exit at the first roundabout and cycle along the Tralee road into Castleisland town. Cycle along Main Street and continue through the traffic lights. Once clear of Castleisland, the houses give way to countryside as the road takes a right turn towards Cordal village at a fork with the Brosna road. The route into Cordal village is very flat with agricultural land dominating the area.

On the approach to Scartaglen.

Soon after passing Cordal church, the road rises very steeply up a thigh-burning hill. The first stage of this climb lasts for 2.5km. Once the worst of the climbing is completed, the road takes a slight ascent into a forested area, before reaching a clearing. Distant views of the road ahead are visible as it drops and rises in an almost roller-coaster style. The initial descent is quite rapid and caution is advised, especially where the road crosses a narrow bridge. In a nutshell, this small area offers four climbs in varying degrees, one after the other. Once all the ups and downs are completed the road soon reaches the junction with the **R577** where the views are quite spectacular. Most of the Kerry mountain ranges can be seen from this spot, (weather permitting) as well as impressive views of the most of the Sliabh Luachra area.

Turn right at the **R577** and travel south-westwards towards Castleisland. For the next 9km enjoy the steady downward descent, well-earned from the previous exertion. As the road nears Scartaglen it crosses the meandering Brown Flesk River in a scene reminiscent of a John Constable painting. Once at the petrol station in Scartaglen take the left-hand road, signposted for Farranfore. This road has a steep and winding descent, once again passing over the river and into Lower Scartaglen. Turn right at the general grocers shop and continue following the signs for Farranfore.

This section of road has a lovely, lively feel to it, with gentle ups and downs that follow the meandering path of the river. Take the road to the right, signposted for Currow, crossing the stone bridge over the Brown

Flesk River. Just beyond the bridge take a left turn and cycle into Currow. For such a small secluded village Currow has a great sporting tradition. It boasts a strong GAA (Gaelic football) club and a healthy cycling tradition, as well as providing Irish rugby with several international players, such as Moss Keane, Mick Galwey and J. J. Hanrahan.

On entering Currow, proceed to the T-junction and turn right onto the **L7006**. As the road leaves the village take the first left turn and continue to a crossroads. Proceed over the **N23**, following the sign for Currans. From here on the road becomes more sheltered, with trees and hedgerows replacing the more open expanses around Currow.

Bear left at the next intersection and enjoy the modest descent into Currans. Follow the road around to the left at the Riverside Inn, under the railway bridge and take the right turn for Tralee. Cross the river once more and get your low gear ready as the road sweeps up sharply to the left. Once on level ground pass over the **N22** and take a right turn at the T-junction. Within 1km this quiet thoroughfare merges with the busy **N22** Tralee-to-Killarney road. Take a left turn and cycle north towards Tralee for no more than 1km, before taking a right turn, signposted for Gortatlea.

Continue down a small hill and over a railway crossing. If you look to the right, it is possible to see the remains of the old Gortatlea railway station. From here on, the road meanders through a small wooded area, before returning to an agricultural terrain. At the T-junction turn right, then left within 20m. From here, O'Riada's Bar is in view. Cross the **N21** to reach your destination.

Right turn for Farranfore.

7. The Three Counties Cycle

Castleisland – Brosna – Three Counties – West Limerick – Feales Bridge – Castleisland

A glimpse of Ireland from bygone years.

Grade: 3/4

Distance: 52.5km

Climbs:

Height gain: 652m

Time: 2½ to 3 hours

Category	Length	Start/End Points	Start/End Elevation	Average Gradient
3	5.34km	3.12km / 8.46km	51m / 251m	3.7%
5	1.62km	18.30km / 19.92km	122m / 211m	5.4%
5	1.8km	26.7km / 28.5km	111m / 171m	3.3%
3	8.2km	38.4km / 46.6km	98m / 247m	1.8%

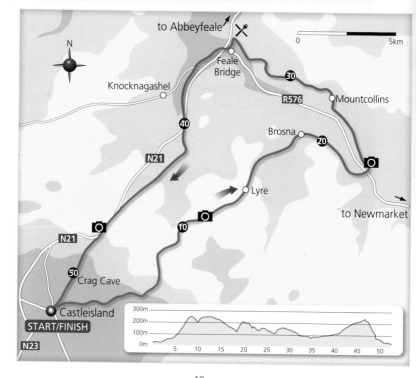

Start/Finish

Castleisland sits quite centrally within Kerry and is a very accessible town. A good starting point for this cycle is the town car park, which is situated in the centre of Castleisland on the Killarney road.

This is a cycle into the old-world side of Kerry. A trip to Brosna is a trip to one of Ireland's highest parishes and a contender for the steepest Main Street! Add to that the magic of Kerry, Cork and Limerick merging at one point, as well as the rolling countryside of the Feale valley in west Limerick. This adds up to over 50km of varied cycling on peaceful country roads.

The descent into Brosna.

Route description

From the car park, follow the one-way system onto Main Street up through the town, continuing straight through the traffic lights. After 1.3km, keep to the left, following the road signposted for Brosna. After the initial flat start to the route, the first climb of the day soon kicks in. This section of the route is quite undisturbed by traffic as well as time. The gradient is very much a minor distraction, as the road passes close to wonderful old farms and small cottages showing off their attractive gardens and bulging turf sheds.

41

The peak of this first climb is at Lyre, a very quiet and remote area. Quickly the route descends, before the road kicks back up to a shorter second climb. By now the road passes through an area thick with trees. Another fast descent sees the route enter the village of Brosna, claimed by many a local to be Ireland's highest parish. It is not difficult to see why, as the Main Street sits on a thigh-burning hill, stretching out beyond the village.

Once through the village, pass by the Brosna GAA grounds to the right and back out into the countryside. This section of road becomes slightly narrower and at times a little uneven, but the eye will be drawn to views of the River Feale down to the left of the route, as it winds through the rich valley towards the coast. Descending towards the aforementioned river, cross the **R576** and go over the bridge. It is close to this point where the Kerry, Cork and Limerick borders meet. The point is marked by a sign in the river and a gazebo-type shelter, erected by the local village committee. Here you will find some useful information about the area as well as an entrance to a short walking trail.

Once over the bridge take the first turning to the left, between two walls that resemble a bridge and proceed in a north-westerly direction, up the small hill and into County Limerick. This narrow road leads to the pretty village of Mountcollins. Pass through the village and follow the signs for the West Limerick Drive. This part of the route is very attractive,

Crossing the Feale near to where the Kerry, Cork and Limerick borders meet.

The steep descent towards Crag Caves.

with rolling countryside, old farmhouses and cottages accompanying the winding road. At 2km outside Mountcollins, take a left at the fork in the road and continue to a T-junction close to Dillane's shop, which sits near the Limerick/Kerry border. This is a good place for refuelling and a toilet break if needed.

From Dillane's, turn left and cycle across the River Feale and back into County Kerry. Keep following what was formerly the old main road between Kerry and Limerick and continue under the new **N21**, keeping to the left. Proceed for approximately 5km to O'Connor's at Headley's Bridge and cycle over the bridge and the River Owveg. Follow the signposts for Tralee and Castleisland as the road starts a gentle climb for about 2km, before finally merging with the **N21**. Continue to the summit.

At the top there is a viewing park, offering great views on a clear day of the MacGillycuddy's Reeks, Carrauntoohil, Tralee Bay, Castleisland and its surrounds. As the road starts to descend, take the left turn, signposted for Crag Cave. As descents go, this is possibly one of steepest in the county. Take care as the road lurches down in two steep sections towards Crag Cave. Be aware of oncoming traffic, especially at the foot of the descent which crosses a narrow bridge. Once that adrenaline rush is over, catch your breath and enjoy the final 3km of very flat road back into Castleisland and the car.

8. Slea Head

Dingle – Ventry – Dunquin – Ballyferriter – Murreagh – Feohanagh – Dingle

A beautiful loop around the best of what the county has to offer in terms of scenery and landmarks.

Grade: 3

Height gain: 603m

Distance: 54km

Time: 1½ to 2½ hours

Climbs:

Category	Length	Start/End Points	Start/End Elevation	Average Gradient
5	2.8km	31.5km / 34.3km	8m / 99m	3.3%
5	3.5km	43km / 46.5km	14m / 101m	2.5%

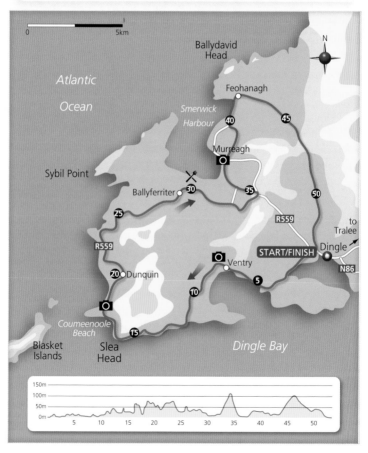

The view of the Atlantic begins to open up after leaving Ventry and heading further out towards Slea Head.

Start/Finish

This route begins in Dingle, which is accessed from the east via the **N86** which you can follow all the way from Tralee via Annascaul and Lispole. There should be ample parking in Dingle, especially in the main car park along the Marina, which is pay and display. There is a also free car park on Spa Road (the Conor Pass exit road out of town) close to the the yellow-painted An Droichead Beag bar.

They often say small can be mighty: this is certainly true for this relatively short route, which offers fantastic value for its length with stunning scenery and Atlantic coastline as well as beautiful landmarks such as Coumeenoole Beach – made famous in the film *Ryan's Daughter* – and Gallarus Oratory, an early Christian church overlooking Smerwick Harbour. This is a cycle that should be high on anyone's bucket list for exploring Kerry and is accessible to everyone.

Please note that the route, although short, is on rolling roads, meaning a good variety of gentle ups and downs. As these roads are unsheltered, they can be subject to some strong Atlantic breezes. However, the route is not too strenuous and is regularly completed by people of all fitness levels and abilities.

Route description

Beginning in Dingle town, go westwards, leaving the Marina and following the **R559**. At the roundabout, follow the sign for the Slea Head Drive, which will lead you in the traditional clockwise direction for the

Heading towards the most westerly point of Slea Head.

duration of this cycle. The first 5km of this route sets the tone nicely for the remainder, in terms of the rolling roads and mountainous views. When you reach Ventry, however, after just 5km, the Atlantic coastline opens up before you, revealing a sight that will make you want to explore more. Ventry is a charming village and has a good beach. Another 3km onwards is Ard a' Bhóthair, the village famous for being the home of the great Kerry footballer Páidí Ó Sé, where there is a statue to commemorate his life and many footballing achievements.

The next section of Slea Head is arguably among the highlights. For approximately the next 10km the road will slowly ascend and meander around the most westerly tip of the peninsula with views of the ocean that make it hard not to want to stop at regular intervals to take it all in. There is a ford at one point that is easily crossed with a little care, but otherwise the road, although narrow, is well enough surfaced for a comfortable journey.

At one point there is a signpost to the beehive huts at Fahan. These are worth a visit and are said to date back to the twelfth century when the Normans forced the native Irish away from good land and towards the periphery of the Dingle Peninsula. The style of dwelling known as the beehive hut (or clochán) dates back a lot earlier, however, with a similar style of corbelling dating back as far as the construction of Newgrange (3100 BC). A set of beehive huts was created on Ceann Sibéal, farther north, between Dunquin and Ballyferriter, to provide a backdrop for the eighth film in the *Star Wars* franchise.

Keep along this road until you reach a signpost for Coumeenoole

Ruins overlooking the Atlantic Ocean and Inis Tuaisceart ('northern island').

Beach. This beach, made famous by the film *Ryan's Daughter* in 1970, has very dramatic views and is worth the slight detour down the ramp off the road to visit it for a short break.

Leaving Coumeenoole, continue for another 10km past Dunquin and towards Ballyferriter. On this section, the road widens significantly. From here, on a clear day, there are magnificent views of the Blasket Islands. Ballyferriter is a small town but very picturesque and might be a good option for a food break as it has a shop and a number of pubs that serve bar food during the day.

Leaving Ballyferriter will mean turning eastwards back towards Dingle. The overall views begin to change dramatically as the ocean scene is replaced by dramatic views of Mount Brandon, which towers in the distance ahead. Not long after leaving Ballyferriter you will see a signpost for Wine Strand to the left. This is an optional detour if you would like to visit the beautiful beach, which has impressive views. Back on the main road, heading towards Dingle and after having completed approximately 35km, you have an option of heading straight back to Dingle (40km in all) or take our recommendation by following signposts for Gallarus Oratory and Murreagh for an additional 10km that is very much worth the effort. Gallarus Oratory is a stone-built early Christian chapel that should not be passed without a visit.

Leaving Gallarus, head north towards Murreagh and along the coastline through Feohanagh. From here, the road rises for arguably the most challenging climb of the day but it is more of a steady slog, at a distance of 3.5km and average gradient of 2.5%, than anything too difficult. At the summit you will have approximately 45km completed and will really appreciate the remaining few kilometres back to the starting point Dingle, which are mostly on a descent.

9. Valentia Island and The Skellig Ring

Cahersiveen – Ballinskelligs – Portmagee – Knightstown – Cahersiveen

A hilly and enjoyable cycle with impressive island and coastal views.

Grade: 3/4

Distance: 56km

Height gain: 733m

Time: 2½ to 3 hours

Climbs:

Category	Length	Start/End Points	Start/End Elevation	Average Gradient
5	3km	22km / 25km	0m / 105m	3%
3	2.5km	30km / 32.5km	18m / 217m	8%
4	8km	40km / 48km	9m / 120m	1%

Start/Finish

This route begins in the town of Cahersiveen in the south-west of the county along the main **N70**, which wraps its way around most of the Iveragh Peninsula. There should be many available parking spaces within the town, with a preferred choice being on Bridge Street, close to the Old Royal Irish Constabulary Barracks where there are also public toilet facilities.

For a relatively short cycle, this route packs a punch for its Atlantic scenery and undulating coastal terrain as well as an opportunity to cycle on the unique and historic Valentia Island, before a return to base via a short ferry trip.

Route Description

Set off from Cahersiveen and head southwards through the town, following directions for Waterville on the **N70** and main Ring of Kerry road. The first 12km or so of the route is mostly on flat terrain, with an occasional rise and fall in the road. Take care as, even though this is a national road, it has a number of potholes and rough patches. Ignore the first two signposts for Ballinskelligs, waiting instead for the turnoff at the 12km mark, taking a right turn onto the **R567**, with a much improved road surface than before. This section of road offers hints of the forthcoming scenery on this route, as the coastline makes brief appearances through infrequent breaks in the

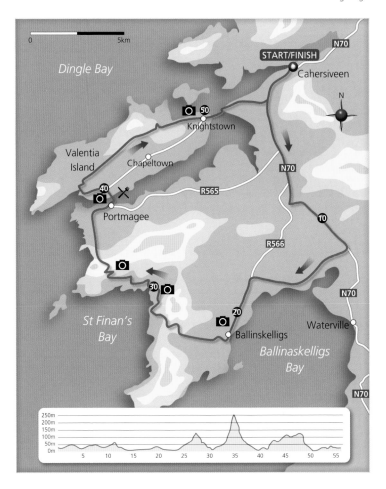

ditches. There is a T-junction at the 18km mark where our route turns left, following signposts for Ballinskelligs, which is 3km further on.

Ballinskelligs is a Gaeltacht village and its name roughly translates as 'Village of the Craggy Rock' and is very popular with visitors who come to the area to enjoy the Blue Flag beach and to immerse themselves in the culture and tranquillity of the area. Beside the beach in Ballinskelligs there is a café and shop as well as toilet facilities and it is a great place to stop and take on some nourishment before some spectacular climbing ahead.

Leaving Ballinskelligs, follow the signposts to the right at a fork in the road for Portmagee and continue along the Skellig Ring. Shortly after this fork in the road the first climb of the day, up to Coom, begins. This climb

Peaceful roads heading towards Ballinskelligs.

has a steady average gradient of 3% and is just under 3km in distance. Descending from Coom there are fantastic views of St Finan's Bay ahead as well the Skellig Islands in the distance. The larger of the two islands, Skellig Michael, which is designated as a UNESCO World Heritage Site, was visible in all its glory in the 2015 Star Wars film *The Force Awakens*, which has boosted tourism and interest in the area significantly. The Skellig Islands will be a prominent feature for much of the remainder of the cycle. At the base of the descent is the home of Skelligs Chocolate Factory and café, which is very difficult to pass without at least a quick peek in the front door.

Well rested and hopefully not too full of chocolate, keep left and head in the direction of Portmagee. From here the climb of Coomanaspic begins, which is the toughest challenge of this route. This is a category 3 climb, just under 2.5km in length, and has a tough average gradient of 8% that only seems to get less forgiving as you approach the top. The final 100m to the summit rises to 20%, leaving a nasty sting in its tail. This is one of the toughest climbs in the county, but the effort is rewarded with breathtaking views of Portmagee and Valentia Island at the summit.

The descent to Portmagee is very fast and rewarding as the cooling breeze refreshes a face reddened from the previous ascent. You will reach the picture-postcard town of Portmagee at the 39km mark. As well as being famous for fishing, Portmagee is also well known as a major departure point for boat trips to the Skellig Islands, which operate in general from mid-May to late September. Cross the bridge, which is clearly visible from the village, and head onto Valentia Island. The bridge, which is the only land link between the island and the mainland, was built in 1970 and named after Maurice O'Neill in memory of a young farmer who was captured and sentenced to death in Dublin in 1942. The house that Maurice O'Neill was lodging in at the time was raided by the Gardaí and after a violent skirmish, Detective George Mordaunt was killed. O'Neill was sentenced to death and executed in November 1942. Crossing the bridge onto Valentia Island has a special appeal, as the route leaves the mainland for a while and there are not too many cycles in that county that can offer that distinction.

After crossing the bridge take the first left and head in an anticlockwise direction around the island on a narrow, well-surfaced road that rises gradually up in the direction of Geokaun mountain before a slow descent towards Knightstown, where you will pass signs for some optional short detours. The first of these is a visit to the Valentia Slate Quarry, from which slate was taken for use in such places as Westminster Abbey and St Paul's Cathedral in London. The second optional detour from this spot travels down to the tetrapod trackway, the earliest record of when four-limbed creatures began to live on dry land. The fossilised footprints are *c.* 370 million years old and one of only four such sites in the world.

Knightstown was once a base of operations for the first transatlantic communications cable, a project begun in the 1860s. The cable ran over 2,730 nautical miles from Valentia to Newfoundland and reduced communication times between Europe and North America from days to

The view from the top of Coomanaspic, with Valentia Island in the background.

minutes. It was a very significant event in global communications at the time. There is a ferry service that offers a regular crossing from Knightstown to Renard Point from 1 April to 30 September. The fare was just €2 for a cyclist to make the 2.5km trip across at the time of writing.

After the ferry journey is complete, leave Renard in an easterly direction before merging with the **N70** once more, taking a left turn at the T-junction and following the route back to Cahersiveen and the starting point of the cycle.

View across to Beginish Island and Cahersiveen Bay from above Knightstown.

10. The Ring of Killarney

Killarney – Lough Guitane – Glenflesk – Barraduff – Anablaha – Kilcummin – Ballyhar – Aghadoe – Killarney

An underrated side of Killarney and its surrounds with beautiful countryside, rolling roads and varied terrain.

Grade: 3/4

Height gain: 607m

Distance: 59km

Time: 2 to 2½ hours

Climbs:

Category	Length	Start/End Points	Start/End Elevation	Average Gradient
5	5.2km	4.2km / 9.4km	23m / 96m	1.4%
5	2.8km	53km / 56km	59m / 109m	1.8%

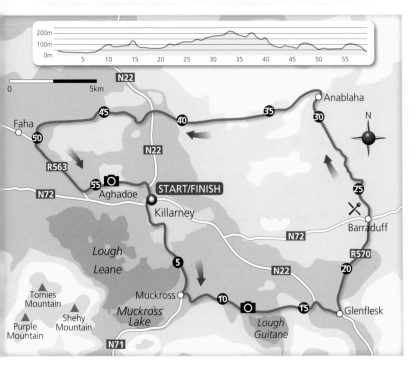

Signpost in Barraduff.

Start/Finish

The Cleeney Roundabout is west of Killarney, where the **N72** and **N22** meet. There should be limited car parking spaces nearby with good access from all directions.

It is fair to say that this route is a little sibling compared to other more popular routes in Killarney, such as the Gap of Dunloe and Moll's Gap; however, this is part of the route's appeal. It has every bit as much scenery and character on roads that are a little quieter and more relaxed. As well as the very pleasant countryside and rolling terrain, there are several focal points along the route, including the freshwater lake at Lough Guitane and the view of Killarney from Aghadoe, which is unmissable.

Route description

Travel along the Dr Hans Liebherr Road (the **N72**). After a short few hundred metres take the second exit on the Ballydowney Roundabout, signposted for the town centre and Kenmare. Follow this road, passing St Mary's Cathedral on your left, considered to be one of the most important Gothic Revival churches in Ireland. Continue onwards, reaching the town centre where the road swings around to the right past the jarvey station and then take a left, signposted for Kenmare and the National Park. This is the beginning of the renowned Muckross Road, the gateway to the fabulous National Park and one of the most popular tourism hotspots in the country.

After 6.5km, follow a signpost for Mangerton to the left, situated just after the Jarvey's Rest Bar and Restaurant. Almost immediately, this quieter road will begin to ascend gradually, with some small climbing efforts throughout that are generally short and punchy with stunning views of Killarney visible behind you. There is a T-junction at the 10km mark where our route turns right. From here the road again rises up towards Lough Guitane, which can be viewed to the right as you ascend. Lough Guitane is one of the freshwater supply sources for much of Kerry. Continue onwards until you reach the main Cork-to-Killarney road (**N22**), turning right towards Cork.

Follow the main road for another 2km until you reach Glenflesk. Here, take a left at the church signposted for Barraduff. A well-surfaced, scenic country road will take you all the way to Barraduff, with a total of 23km now completed. Barraduff might be a good place to stop for a snack or a quick refuel, as there is no shop on the remainder of the route until Killarney. Continue straight on at the crossroads in Barraduff, following signposts for Scartaglen. From here, the beauty of the route becomes apparent, with quiet rural roads that are for the most part well surfaced and no major hills to contend with other than the gentle rise and fall of the natural terrain, which is a characteristic of the entire route in general. Follow this road for the next 4km where you will reach another crossroads and again go straight ahead towards Scartaglen.

The following directions will need to be navigated carefully as they are not very well signposted. The next T-junction is at the 30km mark. Turn right, heading east, but only briefly as the next left turn is just after a small bridge. This leads up to Anablaha school where there is another crossroads. Here, turn left/westwards.

The hills and dales of Sliabh Luachra.

From here, the directions get a little easier as the route follows a straight line via a rolling road past the village of Kilcummin, and on to meet the **N22** after 42km at a crossroads. Continue straight through the crossroads, with care, as it is a busy road, and follow the **L3004** in the direction of Ballyhar. Here the road is quiet; however, the area seems to have a different feel, leaving behind the earlier shrub grounds for lusher and greener pastures. A section of this road runs adjacent to the Tralee-to-Killarney railway line for over 2km. At the next crossroads, continue straight on, following the signpost for Milltown and going straight across the Killarney-to-Firies (**L2019**) crossroads. At the next T-junction, turn left, cycling for just under 1km before merging with the **R563**. Continue left again, in the direction of Killarney, for the next 5km, on a rolling terrain that is easy on the legs and very welcome, as the route sweeps downhill.

At the 54km mark, there is a left turn for Aghadoe and the beginning of a gradual ascent. At the summit of this climb lies Aghadoe Heights Hotel, where there is a large adjacent viewing area offering a good chance to take a breath and enjoy the scenery. The view is very picturesque and offers a wide panorama of scenic beauty, with the Lakes of Killarney to the fore and the towering peaks of the MacGillycuddy's Reeks in the background.

The rest of the route is downhill with two right turns at subsequent T-junctions returning you to Cleeney Roundabout and the starting point.

Descending towards Aghadoe with the Lakes of Killarney in the distance.

11. Annascaul, Minard and Bóthar na gCloch

Camp – Annascaul – Minard – Inch – Bóthar na gCloch – Camp
This route visits a tranquil lake, the village of a famous explorer, a ruined castle and one of Ireland's most famous beaches.

Grade: 3/4

Distance: 62km

Height gain: 915m

Time: 2½ to 3½ hours

Climbs:

Category	Length	Start/End Points	Start/End Elevation	Average Gradient
4	2km	2km / 4.5km	98m / 236m	6%
4	1.4km	25.4km / 26.8km	12m / 103m	6%
3	3km	51.5km / 54.5km	9m / 279m	9%

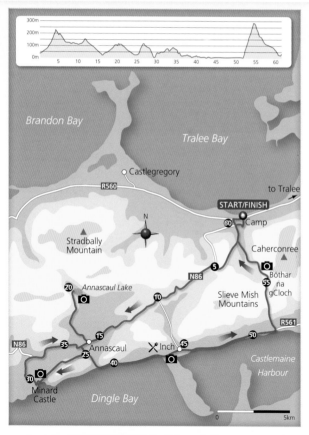

Start/Finish

This route begins in Camp, which is located approximately 16km from Tralee on the **N86**. Camp village itself is quite small; however, there should be parking on the Tralee side of the village across the road from the Railway Tavern and Junction Bar (the two bars are named after the fact that Camp was a popular stop along the Tralee-to-Dingle Light Railway that ran between 1891 and 1953).

The tranquillity of Annascaul Lake.

This is a route for the adventure seeker who wants something a little out of the norm. It takes you away from the main roads for the majority of the cycle, allowing you to explore a little more of what the Dingle Peninsula has to offer. It includes some rewarding climbing as well as areas of scenery, history and immense beauty. There is a category 3 climb included in this route for the return journey to Camp, for those who are up for a challenge. However, an alternative route is described for anybody wanting a more relaxed return to base.

Route description

Beginning at the car park, head west towards a fork in the road. Take the left-hand option and follow signposted directions for Annascaul. Just before Ashe's Pub in Camp turn left onto a quiet country road. After approximately 1km follow a sign to the right, heading for the Dingle Way. Here is the beginning of the first climb of the day on a road known locally as the Old

Bog Road. Easier gears and a sensible, paced approach is recommended to this climb, as it can drag on a little with legs that have not yet warmed up, but at the summit its rewards will be evident in the panoramic views of mountain, countryside and ocean. Only a few short kilometres into this cycle and already the landscape is markedly different than at the starting point. After the summit of this climb the roads sweeps quickly down and onwards, but be sure to keep right until eventually meeting the main **N86**, where we turn left, heading in the direction of Annascaul.

The road to Annascaul is undulating but pacey, with the majority of the distance being on a descent. You will reach the village with approximately 16km completed. There are a number of shops in Annascaul if refuelling is needed; however, this may be a bit early for a break. In the middle of the village, adjacent to the South Pole Inn, follow directions to the right for Ballynacourty and Anagap. The South Pole Inn is a bar and restaurant once owned and run by the Antarctic explorer Tom Crean and his wife, Ellen. Crean went to the Antarctic with expeditions led by both Scott and Shackleton in the early 1900s. The South Pole Inn is still open and, as well as a serving drinks and food, also has a museum and gift shop dedicated to Tom's life and adventures.

After taking a right at the South Pole Inn, continue along this road and follow directions for Annascaul Lake, passing a signpost along the way for an optional short detour to Tom Crean's resting place in Ballynacourty Graveyard. Close to the lake the road surface begins to worsen in parts. Continue until meeting a gate on the road which has an entrance to the side of it, from where the road sweeps down to the lakeside. Annascaul Lake, nestled in between mountains and folklore, is one of the highlights of this route and an excellent place to take a break and have a food stop, having completed roughly 20km so far. Legend has it that Annascaul Lake was formed when two mighty giants, one of them said to have been Cú Chulainn, fought a battle for the hand of the fair maiden Scaul.

Leaving the lake, retrace your route back to Annascaul and when you reach the village, take a right-hand turn where you will rejoin the **N86**. After only a few hundred metres, turn left, following signposts for Inch and Killarney. You are now on the **R561** but only for a short while: take the first right on this road, which brings on the second climb of the day. This climb is only a distant relation of the day's first effort and is more steady than sharp. After completing the climb you will sweep down towards the coastline again and towards Minard Castle, having completed 30km. The substantial ruins of the castle sit prominently overlooking a storm beach, with impressive views of the Iveragh Peninsula. It was built in the mid-sixteenth century by the Fitzgeralds and partially destroyed by Cromwellian forces in 1650.

Continue on this road for approximately 1km, where a right turn will eventually bring you back onto the **N86** at a T-junction. Turn right here

The ruins of Minard Castle.

and continue until you reach a familiar turnoff to the right, cycling onto the **R561**, following signposts for Inch and Killarney. Keep on this stretch of road for the next 6km with impressive views of the ocean and Iveragh Peninsula for company as Inch Beach draws nearer. Inch Beach is 5km long and, with its Blue Flag status, is popular year round with swimmers, beach walkers and water-sports enthusiasts. It also served as the backdrop for two films, *Ryan's Daughter* and *The Playboy of the Western World* and, with the setting it has, it is easy to understand why it was chosen. There is a café and shop at the entrance to the beach and this would be a good place to take some rest, with 45km completed so far.

The last part of your journey now begins. Leaving Inch, continue along the **R561** for another 7km where there is a signpost pointing left for the Scenic Route to Camp and The Maharees. From here begins the third and final climb of the day: it is the south–north approach to Bóthar na gCloch, which is a 3km category 3 climb with an average gradient of 9%. It has an ominous look about it but with an easy gear, a little patience and grit, this climb is surmountable. It starts rather gently but the gradient gradually increases towards the top. Do not forget during this climb, or possibly at the top, to stop and look behind you to appreciate the benefits of your efforts. You will reach the summit of this climb with 58km completed and just a short descent remaining to take you back to Camp. The descent itself is quite steep at the very start, so take care. Also there is a fork in the road on the descent: both roads will eventually get you back to Camp village but the left option is the direct route. You will reach Camp having completed 62km.

Please note: If the final climb of the day feels a little too much, an alternative would be to retrace the journey back into Annascaul and Camp via the **N86**.

A welcome food stop at Inch Beach.

The majesty of Bóthar na gCloch.

12. King Puck Route

Milltown – Beaufort – Kilgobnet – Lough Caragh – Killorglin – Callanafersy – Milltown

Peaceful laneways and roads, set against a stunning Carrauntoohil backdrop.

Grade: 3

Distance: 62km

Climbs: No major climbs on this route

Height gain: 428m

Time: 3 to 4 hours

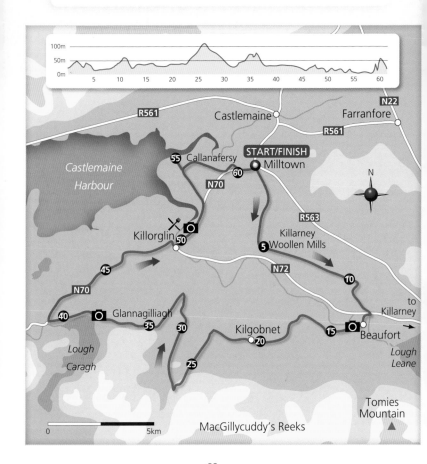

Beaufort Bridge.

Start/Finish

The route starts in the mid-Kerry village of Milltown which is a 20km drive from both Tralee and Killarney. Parking should not be a problem in Milltown with a good option being at the Castlemaine end of the village, close to the post office.

A perfect route for cyclists who like the quieter side of life. On offer are single-track lanes, leafy village roads, stunning mountain views and glimpses of the impressive Caragh Lake. This route caters for anyone not in the mood for the big climbs, but with the options of the shorter challenging hills.

Route description

Leaving the start point, cycle on the **N70** in the direction of Killorglin. Follow the bend in the road and the climb out of the village. Take the first left turn onto the road signposted Lyre/Recycling Centre. This section of road is relatively flat and the runs through a rural and rugged landscape, with scattered woodland, hedgerows and small bungalows. After 4.4km from Milltown, take the left turn at the second crossroads, heading east. The road is unmarked, but known locally as the Kerry Woollen Mills road.

The terrain in this area remains similar to the previous stretch but with a more agricultural feel. Continue eastwards for 2.5km; proceed straight over the crossroads, on a road called Lahard Cottages. At this point the

A hill near Kilgobnet.

road narrows slightly and the surface becomes a little uneven. The route reaches a T-junction at Faha Glen. Turn right and continue on as the road descends steadily towards the **N72** Ring of Kerry route. On reaching the T-junction with the **N72**, turn right and cycle for a short distance before taking the first left towards Beaufort. Cycle over the eye-catching stone bridge before taking the first road to the right, signposted for Killorglin and Beaufort Golf Club. Continue on through this neat little village before passing by the entrance to Beaufort Golf Club, 2.5km on. Take the left turn, signposted Churchtown burial grounds, and continue along this attractive leafy stretch of road before crossing the stone bridge that straddles the River Gaddagh. From here on the panorama opens up, with distant mountain views of Carrauntoohil over to the south-west. Enter the village of Kilgobnet and proceed straight through, keeping very much to the left at the fork at the far end of the village. This next stretch of road is initially quite narrow as it bypasses small dwellings and farmsteads, continuing over another stone bridge before arriving at Shannera Cross approximately 2km from Kilgobnet. This crossroads is unmarked. Take the left turn between the grotto and an old white house and proceed up a steady climb. This stretch of the route cuts through a forested area with great views of Carrauntoohill as the road levels out. From here, the route meanders down to meet the Glencar-to-Killorglin road, where we turn right. Continue for 1km in a south-westerly direction before reaching a unique road sign that points the way to eight different destinations. Take the right turn for Killorglin, scaling up another steady climb for 6km. This area is quite barren but gives off a warm golden glow in the sunshine as the road rises gently through scrub and bogland.

Once at the next major crossroads, indicated by the sign for Ardrahan House B&B, take the left turn for Cappanalea and enjoy a steady 2.5km descent. At the next T-junction, take the right turn. Avoid at all costs the steep hill and the left-hand road sign pointing to Cappanalea. Along this section, the road narrows and passes through a fairly densely wooded area. This soon gives way to a few twists and turns, before merging onto a T-junction close to Glannagilliagh National School. Take the left turn and go straight past the small general shop, in the direction of Carrig Country House and Glenbeigh.

On this section of the road Caragh Lake can be seen to the left, close to the entrance to Carrig Country House. This area is dominated by plush-looking properties stretching back from the roadway on tree-lined avenues. Take the right turn by the sign at the entrance to Glendalough Country House and continue up to the next T-junction. Take a right turn onto the **N70** and take the main Ring of Kerry road into Killorglin for approximately 6km.

Killorglin is famous for its Puck Fair. The fair, dating back to 1603, takes place every August and brings vast crowds into the town. The centrepiece is a puck (male) goat that is captured in the nearby mountains prior to the fair. It is kept high above the town on a large platform for the duration of the fair before being set free. Killorglin is an ideal place to grab a well-earned break and a bite to eat. The town has pubs, cafés and shops in abundance.

Passing through Killorglin, follow the signs for Tralee and proceed over the impressive Laune Bridge. At the mini-roundabout take the first exit for Tralee and continue on the **N70** for 3km. Take the left turn for Callanafersy and follow the straight, narrow road down to the pier and slipway. From here it is worth pausing for a few minutes to take in the views of Castlemaine harbour, the Slieve Mish Mountains and Inch Strand. In the last century this was the disembarkation point for a small ferry which ran between Callanafersy and Keel on the opposite bank. One of the ferry's main purposes was the transportation of livestock from the Castlemaine area to the market at Killorglin.

Retrace the route for 1km and take the unmarked road to the left. The landscape swiftly changes from open farmland to forest with the road running very straight and flat. Proceed up the slight incline through a canopy of trees and rejoin the **N70** close to Milltown. Take the left turn up the hill and pass the cemetery, before dropping down into Milltown and back to the starting point.

13. Priest's Leap and The Borlin Valley

Kenmare – Priest's Leap – Coomhola Bridge – Borlin Valley – Kilgarvan – Kenmare

A rite-of-passage route on tough mountainous terrain.

Grade: 4/5			Height gain: 1,050m	
Distance: 65km			Time: 3½ to 4 hours	

Climbs:

Category	Length	Start/End Points	Start/End Elevation	Average Gradient
2	3.5km	13km / 16.5km	140m / 440m	9%
3	7.5km	30km / 37.5km	60m / 340m	4%

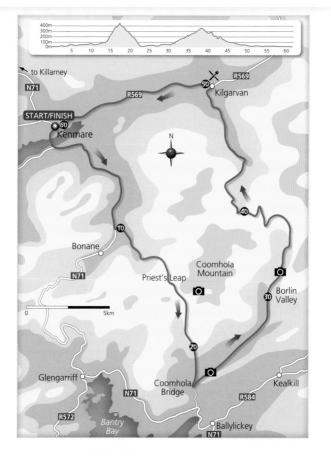

Start/Finish

This route begins in Kenmare where there should be ample parking in the town. There is also a public car park opposite Kenmare Holy Cross church just off the main square.

There should be medals and certificates handed out at the end of this route! They will seem well deserved after two hard climbs in the middle of a cycle that meanders over the Cork border and back again into Kerry on a mettle-testing expedition that tries even the most experienced of cyclists. The reward, however, is a countryside full of character that almost feels unexplored and most certainly will not be overly busy with either bicycle or motor traffic. Please note that some areas of the route, particularly on the descent of the Priest's Leap, require full attention as the surface is less than perfect in parts. Be sure to bring provisions as there is no planned stop at a shop or café en route.

Route description

Leave Kenmare and head southwards on the **N71**, crossing Our Lady's Bridge and follow signposts for Glengarriff along a rolling road for approximately 10km. Just before reaching the picturesque village of Bonane follow a signpost to the left for the Priest's Leap. Shortly after, take a right at a fork on the road, again well signposted for the Priest's Leap. This road is a distinct change from the previous one and, although evenly

A serene country road just before the hardest part of the Priest's Leap ascent begins.

The view from the top of the Priest's Leap, with Bantry Bay in the distance.

surfaced, it is narrower and has a grassy centre. From here the gradual ascent of the Priest's Leap begins, with pleasant farmland and countryside to admire on both sides of the road. The area is said to have got its unusual place name after a priest made a miraculous leap from here while being pursued by English soldiers. After a small bridge, the severity of the ascent changes and very noticeably so. For the next 3.5km there will be a lot of convincing both bike and body to respond as the climb rises to 17% in parts with only one reprieve along the way up, where you can comfortably stop for a moment and catch your breath. Do not be surprised if some of the climb requires walking. The summit of the climb appears after 16.5km of cycling with views of Bantry Bay and Whiddy Island visible before you in the distance on a clear day. As you begin your descent you will cross the border into County Cork.

The next 6km of descent to Coomhola will be a welcome relief and a respite for the legs; however, it is quite technical with some steep sections, so caution is advised to keep close control of your brakes. You will reach Coomhola Bridge with approximately 23km on the clock. This is a good place to stop and take on some food and liquid and reflect on having just completed the hardest part of today's cycle.

When ready to head off again on the opposite side of the bridge, take an immediate left, following the signpost for Borlin. If there is any opportunity to get lost on this route it is here as there are signposts highlighting bike trails in many directions, so take a moment to make sure you are following the right one. The next 7.5km begins the gradual ascent up towards the Borlin Valley and, unlike the previous climb of the day, this one is a lot more forgiving as it eases you gently into a steady gradient for the length of the climb, with remarkable views of the Borlin Valley to your left as you climb. This climb has similarities with parts of the south–north approach of Moll's Gap. The summit is visible high up to your left for a long time and looks quite daunting at first, but it gets nearer with every turn of the pedals and you will reach the summit at the 37.5km mark, with panoramic views ahead and behind.

For the next 10km a feeling of elation will accompany you on a stunning descent back into County Kerry and the village of Kilgarvan, as the two hard climbs of the day have been conquered. Kilgarvan will be a welcome sight as you reach a T-junction and take a left onto the **R569** in the direction of Kenmare. In Kilgarvan there is a petrol station with a shop. The remainder of this cycle continues along the **R569** and back towards Kenmare on well-surfaced roads, which should feel easier on the legs despite some tiredness from the day's efforts. You will reach Kenmare having completed 65km. Take a right down through the town and back again to the car park.

The gradual ascent of the Borlin Valley.

14. North Kerry Hurling Tour

Ballyheigue – Ardfert – Kilflynn – Ballyduff – Causeway – Ballyheigue

Wandering from village to village through north Kerry's hurling centre.

Grade: 2/3

Height gain: 388m

Distance: 68km

Time: 3 to 3½ hours

Climb: No climbs major climbs on this route

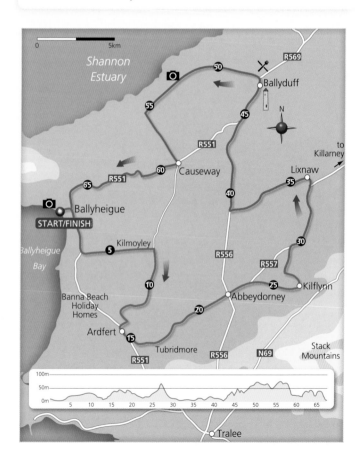

The starting point in Ballyheigue.

Start/Finish

This route begins in the centre of Ballyheigue, which lies 18km north of Tralee, along the **R551**. A good place to park is just in front of Ballyheigue Castle in the centre of the village or alternatively close to the beachfront. There are shops and public toilets in the vicinity.

Gaelic football is arguably Ireland's premier sport, with Kerry undoubtedly its most successful team. The other major Gaelic sport, hurling, is also very much alive and kicking in the Kingdom of Kerry. This route travels through the hurling heartland of north Kerry, touching base with the key villages. This area is generally overlooked by tourists, as they travel either to the south or west in pursuit of the better-known towns and attractions. That is very much their loss, as this area of north Kerry presents a rich history, beauty and character that are peerless.

Route description

Leaving the starting point, cycle east away from the ocean. At the T-junction of the **R551** take a right turn towards Tralee and Ardfert. This first section of road travels through a marshy area and is very flat, with fine views of the Banna Strand sand dunes to the right.

After about 3km take a left turn, signposted Kilmoyley and go along a slightly narrower and quieter road, which leads straight through the heart of the village. The actual village centre is very small and is identified by the large Sacred Heart church to the right and An Tochair Bán pub across the road. Proceed through the village and turn right at next T-junction. Continue through Lerrig Cross, following an S-bend up a modest hill. Continue on to the medieval village of Ardfert, passing St Brendan's GAA hurling field to the left on the outskirts of the village. The standout feature of the village is Ardfert Cathedral. Dating from the twelfth century, the cathedral is dedicated to St Brendan the Navigator. Much of the site has been restored in recent times and is well worth a visit for the ambience and craftsmanship on offer.

From the cathedral proceed southwards to the **R551**. At the filling station turn left onto Station Road. This leads through a more residential area of the village before returning to countryside. At the crossroads at Tubridmore, turn left onto the **L2009** and continue to Abbeydorney. This road, although relatively flat, has a few small hills, but nothing too strenuous. If you look closely, you may notice some traces of the old railway track that once ran alongside the road to the right. It was once part of the Tralee-to-Limerick line, which was closed in the late 1970s. At the crossroads of the **R556/R557** cycle straight across onto the **R557** in the direction of Listowel. In little over 1km from Abbeydorney, the road crosses a small bridge. Take the immediate right turn for Kilflynn and follow a straight and charming tree-lined road to the village centre.

On entering the village of Kilflynn you come to a crossroads with St Mary's church to your right. Turn left and cycle up the hill towards St Teresa's National School. At the fork in the road just beyond the school, take the right turn and cycle downhill. At Crotta Woods the road appears to split. Take the left-hand option. At the next stop sign take another left turn before emerging at the junction of the **R557** Listowel-to-Abbeydorney road. Turn right here towards Listowel.

Continue on to the next village: Lixnaw. On entering the village take a left turn into the centre of the village. At the top of the village follow the road around to the left and cycle for approximately 5km to the **R556** intersection. Turn right towards Ballyduff and Ballybunion. Prior to reaching Ballyduff, it might be worth an off-road excursion to visit the Rattoo round tower. The tower dates from about 1100, with the ruins of a fifth-century church and graveyard close by. The tower can be spotted to the right off the **R556**. This excursion will add little more than 1km onto the journey.

The road into Ballyduff has a few twists and turns and a slight incline before levelling out once inside the village. Ballyduff is a good place to stop as it has a couple of shops that serve the needs of a hungry and thirsty cyclist. Proceed through the village and take the left turn onto the road signposted Causeway and Coast Road.

Generally, this section of road is quite flat and exposed but does offer some spectacular views of the County Clare and Ballybunion coastlines to the north. After approximately 8km from Ballyduff, turn left for Causeway at Meenogahane crossroads. This can be identified by an old bungalow close by. The cycle into Causeway starts quite flat, but ends in a steepish descent on Farran Hill. Caution is advised as the descent is very fast and merges very quickly with a crossroads in Causeway. Turn right at the crossroads and head towards Ballyheigue. As you leave the village, the hurling pitch can be seen to the left, followed quickly by the modern Dairymaster factory to the right.

The cycle back to Ballyheigue is certainly not boring on this final stretch of road. Enjoy the scenery: fertile green fields falling down to the left, a panorama of the Slieve Mish mountains further on in the distance and finally views of the coast as the route nears its conclusion at Ballyheigue. This final section offers a few twists and turns as well as challenging small hills that keep things interesting. The final climb of the day concludes on a hilltop where the imposing local church stands. From here, enjoy a fast descent past the grotto before a right turn at the foot of the hill that leads back into Ballyheigue.

Kilflynn village.

15. Killarney to Tralee: the Hidden Roads

Firies – Killarney – Currow – Farmer's Bridge – Tralee – Ballyfinnane – Firies

A Killarney-to-Tralee circuit off the beaten track.

Grade: 3

Distance: 68km

Height gain: 739m

Time: 3 to 4 hours

Climbs:

Category	Length	Start/End Points	Start/End Elevation	Average Gradient
3	8.4km	18.6km / 27km	45m / 196m	1.7%
5	3.2km	38km / 41.2km	21m / 90m	2.1%
4	6.7km	53.3km / 60km	4m / 175m	2.5%

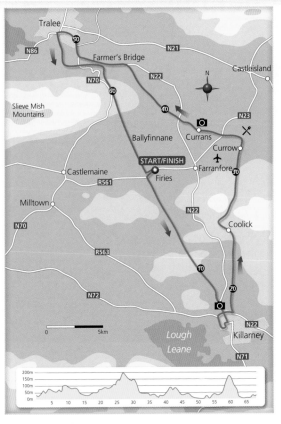

Start/Finish

This route begins in a very central part of the county, in Firies village, which is pretty much equidistant between Tralee to the north and Killarney to the south. Firies is just 4km from Farranfore. Take the **N22** from either Tralee or Killarney; on reaching Farranfore, take the **R561** to Firies. There are plenty of places to park in Firies with ample space near the church, which is just off the main road, to the right as you enter the village.

Ballyfinnane village.

The Tralee-to-Killarney route is now dominated by the busy **N22** which will get you between the two towns in under thirty minutes by car or bus. Step back in time to the nineteenth and early twentieth centuries and enjoy the type of route our forefathers would have travelled. Unearth an adventure on the quiet country lanes running no more than a kilometre or two from the busy main thoroughfare.

Route description

Cycle out of Firies onto the **R561** towards Castlemaine and Killorglin. Once through the village proceed onto the **L2019** road, following the Ballyhar and Killarney signposts. This road runs directly into Killarney. There is one major climb on this stretch near Ballyhar. Interestingly, it starts with a fast descent that traverses the railway line, a crossroads and the River Gweestin in quick succession before sweeping up towards a steep climb of 600m. When the road finally reaches the turning for Aghadoe Heights

Hotel, continue down the hill before turning right onto the busy **N22** and continue into Killarney. At the Cleeney Roundabout take first exit for Cork and the **N22**. At the next junction turn left onto the Kilcummin Road. This takes you immediately into countryside and away from the town. There is a tricky little hill to negotiate with a double bend: be careful of oncoming traffic and a broken road surface. At the crossroads at the top of the hill, continue straight across. The area is made up mainly of agricultural land and small bungalows and individual houses. At the next crossroads (Finnegan's Cross), continue in the same northerly direction, following the sign for Coolick National School. Along this stretch of road the terrain gets a bit more interesting as the road falls and then kicks up a sheltered hill. Continue past the sign for Coolick. About 1.3km after the Coolick turn take the right turn, signposted for Currow.

This stretch climbs steeply up and around a steady bend. The road at this point is quite narrow, so be aware of oncoming traffic. As the area levels out the trees and bushes give way to a bog landscape. The area has little or no housing and feels quite remote. Very quickly normality is restored with at first a gentle descent and glimpses of Farranfore Airport to the left. The gentle descent is soon replaced by a steep hill that twists its way down onto the Scartaglen-to-Farranfore road. Cross this road and continue into Currow. With a couple of general shops, Currow could very well be the ideal place for a coffee break. Continue on through the village before taking the first left turn onto the **L7006**, distinguished by a smart-looking sign and garden welcoming people into Currow. On reaching the junction with the **N23**, continue straight across, following the signpost for Currans. At the next junction turn left and continue into Currans village. Passing the Riverside Inn, take the right turn under the railway bridge, signposted for Tralee.

Continue over the bridge and follow the road up the hill, crossing the **N22** road bridge. At the crossroads follow the Ballyfinnane sign and continue for 500m. At a sign for Hickey's Nurseries, take the road to the right, which has tufts of grass down the centre.

For the next 8km this road will lead to the outskirts of Tralee via Farmer's Bridge. Although quite narrow and at times wide enough for just one motorised vehicle, the surface rides quite well. Small areas of the road surface are broken, but these are mainly confined to the first kilometre. Expect a rolling surface with one or two gentle hills as well as cheery wave from many of the locals who live nearby.

On entering Farmer's Bridge crossroads, ride over the small bridge and continue straight on. Follow what is now an improved road surface to the next right turn. This is unmarked and is identified by a STOP sign on the road surface. Turn right and follow the road around until it reaches the junction with the **N70**. Take the right turn and proceed to Tralee. At the roundabout after Lidl take the first exit onto the **N86**. Continue on this

Currans. Nice spot for a break!

road, passing straight through the Ballymullen Roundabout and continue on to the next roundabout adjacent to the Aquadome.

Note: *To visit the centre of Tralee, take the third exit at the roundabout, which is distinguished by a fountain, and continue past the Brandon Hotel on your left. From here on, you are in the centre of the town.*

Take the left turn for Ballyard on the **L2010** and continue over the railway tracks and up the hill. Follow the road out of Tralee and past the rugby club. At the T-junction, turn left. Continue for just over 1km to a crossroads. Go straight across and continue on the **L2012** for Caherleheen. This road leads back to Farmer's Bridge and at the crossroads follow the road around to the right. Almost immediately the route starts to climb. The road is named Lisard Heights and it is one of the most respected road climbs within the Tralee area. After a leg-sapping 2km/130m climb, enjoy the nice, straight but speedy descent into Ballyfinnane. Pass by The Shanty pub and continue straight through the crossroads, following the Firies sign. From here it is just 5km back to the starting point. At the next junction, turn left back into the centre of Firies village and to your starting point.

16. The Gap of Dunloe and The Black Valley

Gap of Dunloe – Black Valley – Lough Brin – Moll's Gap – Killarney – Gap of Dunloe

Kerry at its best and most scenic with little or no traffic: not to be missed.

Grade: 4			Height gain: 1,076m	
Distance: 73km			Time: 3½ to 4 hours	
Climbs:				
Category	Length	Start/End Points	Start/End Elevation	Average Gradient
4	5.5km	0km / 5.5km	61m / 224m	3%
3	11km	10.5km / 21.5km	29m / 256m	2%
3	8.5km	28.5km / 37km	75m / 272m	2%
5	2.7km	50km / 52.5km	24m / 87m	2%

Start/Finish

From Killarney town centre take the **N72**/Killorglin road and follow signs for the Gap of Dunloe, stopping just 10km outside the town at Kate Kearney's Cottage where there is lots of parking, as well as food and last-minute supplies if needed.

The Gap of Dunloe and the Black Valley are among the most renowned areas for tourists in Kerry and with good reason. The glacial landscape appears timeless and for the most part untouched by modern life. The majority of the route is on quiet roads with little traffic and ample opportunity to soak up the surrounds, including views of Lakes of Killarney, the MacGillycuddy's Reeks, Purple Mountain, Ladies View and Muckross Park. The surface for most of the route is as good as you would hope for in a remote area such as this; however, caution is required in one or two areas. This route is relatively short but due to the varied terrain and some challenging climbs it is a good idea to begin the cycle with plenty of provisions as options for buying food are located only at the start and towards the end of the cycle.

Route description

Head in the direction of the Gap of Dunloe from Kate Kearney's Cottage. At the beginning this might seem like a busy route with potentially lots of

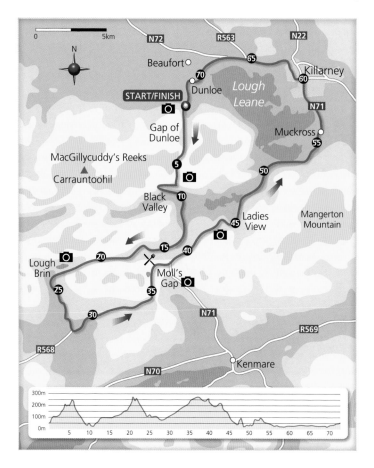

activity from jarveys, tourists and walkers; however, after only a few short kilometres there should be very little traffic. The initial ascent leads up to a bridge in between the first two lakes of the day. This bridge is known as the Wishing Bridge and wishes made on it are supposed to come true. Continue along the Gap of Dunloe where the terrain will dip and rise in several areas alongside glacial rocks and lakes until the road reaches a sign for the Black Valley and it is here that the second part of the journey begins as the road rolls downwards on a quick descent. About 2km into the descent take a left at a fork in the road and on past the church, heading further into the valley.

After another kilometre there is a fork in the road. Our route follows the path to the right; however, an optional detour to the left leads on towards Lord Brandon's Cottage which was built in the nineteenth century and

In the heart of the Gap of Dunloe alongside Augher Lake.

primarily used as a hunting lodge. In the summer months it is open during the day as a restaurant and also provides a quick return to Killarney via a boat trip to Ross Castle, which is another option for a shortened version of the route. Bikes can be carried on the boats, depending on capacity and the price for the boat trip is approximately €15.

The next 8km are right in the heart of the Black Valley and are on mostly flat or rolling roads with plentiful picnic spots on riverbanks and opportunities to soak in the surroundings, some of which are lush and green while others seem scorched and quite dry in summer. The remoteness of this area is underlined by the fact that it was the last place in Ireland to receive electrification.

With approximately 17km completed, take a right at a fork in the road (ignoring signpost directions for Killarney and Kenmare) onto a smaller road. This section of road is a bit narrower and rougher than what has been covered up to now, but as it ascends, views of Lough Brin and Ballaghbeama mountain pass in the distance are breathtaking. Continue on a descent, with Lough Brin on the right, and follow the road as it sweeps left and along a well-surfaced section until you meet a crossroads where the route turns left onto the **R568**. From here the road deadens slightly and becomes hard to pedal on as it makes it way gradually up towards Moll's Gap.

Shortly before Moll's Gap is the Strawberry Field Pancake Cottage, which serves excellent savoury and sweet pancakes as well as tea and coffee, and there is always a fire lit on a cold day. There is also a café at Moll's Gap itself with more ample seating to cater for a larger crowd. Either of these is ideal for a stop and reflection on the terrain just covered. The view from Moll's Gap is a good indication of the road to come with Killarney with its lakes nestled in the distance beneath.

Cycling alongside Black Lough, the last body of water before entering the Black Valley.

The grassy roads between the Black Valley and Lough Brin.

From Moll's Gap follow signposts for Killarney on the **N71** as the road makes its way mostly downwards, along with one or two surprise short rises. There are several spots along the way that have marvellous views of Killarney's lakes, among them Ladies View, Torc Waterfall and Muckross House and Gardens. Approaching Killarney town, follow signposts for Killorglin and Ring of Kerry (**N72**). On leaving Fossa, turn left, following the brown signs marked for the Gap of Dunloe, which will bring you back to Kate Kearney's Cottage and the start of your journey.

17. The Lacey Cup Circuit

Tralee – Camp – Annascaul – Inch – Keel – Castlemaine – Tralee

A favourite circuit with local cycling clubs and tourists in the know.

Grade: 3/4

Distance: 74km

Height gain: 662m

Time: 3 to 3½ hours

Climbs:

Category	Length	Start/End Points	Start/End Elevation	Average Gradient
3	5.03km	14.82km / 19.85km	33m / 199m	3.3%
3	5.40km	60.38km / 65.78km	8m / 172m	3%

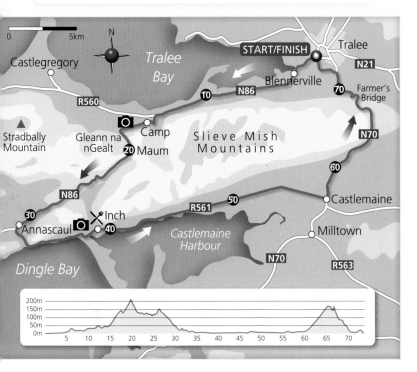

Start/Finish

This is a very accessible route that can be started from any point in Tralee. For the easiest access we recommend starting close to the Tralee Aquadome. This is near the start of the **N86** on the western side of the town. There is ample parking near here and immediate access to the **N86**, which is the gateway to the west.

The Lacey Cup is the name of a national cycle race run each year from Tralee in the spring. This circuit traces the exact route of the race. Tralee is where north Kerry meets west Kerry in a fusion of wild Atlantic scenery on either side of the Slieve Mish Mountains on the Dingle Peninsula. Experience two exhilarating climbs, stunning ocean views, charming villages, long sweeping white beaches, wildlife in abundance and the freshest of sea and mountain air.

Route description

On leaving Tralee take the **N86** alongside the Blennerville–Tralee canal and go through Blennerville village. The route continues on to the main Dingle road, which is as straight as an arrow, with a few small hills thrown in to keep the traveller on their toes. To the right, there are fine views of Tralee Bay, Fenit and the Maharees. To the left, the area is shadowed by the

The top of Gleann na Gealt looking across Tralee Bay towards Kerry Head.

Looking towards Mount Brandon from the top of Gleann na Gealt.

Slieve Mish Mountains. These mountains will be in close attendance for the whole of this cycle.

Things become interesting as the route nears Camp village. Follow the **N86** off to the left towards Camp and Annascaul. From here on, there is a steady climb through Camp village and up towards Gleann na nGealt.

The name Gleann na nGealt translates into English as 'The Valley of the Mad'. Local folklore mentions that a cure for madness exists in the area. Interestingly here, some naturally occurring traces of lithium were found in local water samples, so this old wives' tale may have a hint of truth in it after all.

The climb itself is very steady and far easier than the 5km length may suggest. On reaching the summit at Maum, you will be rewarded with spectacular views out towards Mount Brandon and Castlegregory. The downward stretch passes mainly through sheep-farming territory and into Annascaul village. This pretty west Kerry village is famed as the birthplace of Tom Crean, the twentieth-century Antarctic explorer. His pub, The South Pole Inn, lies to the west side of the village. The inside of the pub has a museum feel about it, with many pictures and artefacts adorning the bar area, detailing some of the great man's expeditions. On leaving Annascaul take the left-hand road **R561** towards Inch. This is arguably the nicest stretch of the ride. The road follows the Annascaul River to its mouth at Bunaneer, before the road turns eastwards and follows a spectacular ocean ride that continues beyond Inch.

Inch Strand is always worth a stop and, after 38km in the saddle, it might just be the place for a well-earned break. The 5km stretch of beach gained fame after parts of the 1970 blockbuster film *Ryan's Daughter* were shot in the location. The beach is now a very popular destination with surfers and walkers alike.

Continue along the **R561** where the views are still excellent, with the mountains rising to the left and clear views of Cromane, across Castlemaine harbour, to the right. The road at this point is very straight and most of the route into Castlemaine consists now of small, rolling hills interspersed by flat sections.

On entering Castlemaine, take a left at the T-junction onto the **N70**, following the signpost for Tralee. This leads out of the village onto a flat section of road. Within 3km the final climb of the day begins. This leads over the tail end of the Slieve Mish Mountains towards Tralee. The climb is steady and lasts for approximately 5km. The downward section is of a similar distance and contains two technical hairpin bends, which add some excitement to the final few kilometres. As the road levels out, follow the straight section into Tralee before taking a left at the roundabout after Lidl. The starting point at the Aquadome is less than 2km away towards the end of the Dan Spring Road.

R561 road near Inch.

18. Cromane, Rossbeigh and Caragh Lake

Killorglin – Cromane – Glenbeigh – Rossbeigh – Glenbeigh – Caragh Lake – Glencar – Killorglin

A showcase of the best of the county's natural landscape.

Grade: 3/4			Height gain: 756m	
Distance: 73.5km			Time: 3 to 3½ hours	
Climbs:				
Category	Length	Start/End Points	Start/End Elevation	Average Gradient
4	1.5km	27km / 28km	4m / 144m	9%
5	5.1km	44km / 49km	16m / 81m	1.3%
4	10km	51.3km / 61.4km	26m / 167m	1.4%

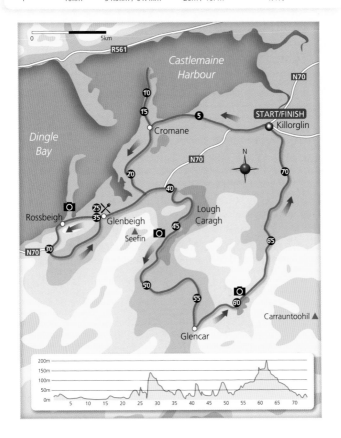

Heading towards Cromane Pier with the Dingle Peninsula in the background.

Start/Finish

This route begins in Killorglin town centre on the **N70** where there is a big pay-and-display car park in front of the church and ample shops in the vicinity to stock up for the road ahead.

This is a cycle that offers great variety within the gateway to the Iveragh Peninsula and the famous Ring of Kerry. It begins with two locations, Cromane and Rossbeigh, that have stunning views of the Atlantic Ocean and the Dingle Peninsula. It then ventures inland from Glenbeigh towards Glencar and Caragh Lake. Here is a more serene and sheltered setting, with a backdrop of lakes, forested areas, wild bogland and the MacGillycuddy's Reeks, before returning you back to Killorglin, which itself has a very long history and association with cycling. With routes like this on its doorstep, it is easy to appreciate why.

Route description

Leaving Killorglin take the **N70**, signposted for Glenbeigh and the Ring of Kerry, for two rolling kilometres until reaching a signpost for Cromane to the right. Follow this road for another 6km to the village when you meet a T-junction with an imposing church to the left-hand side. Cromane is a small rural fishing village with fantastic views of the Dingle Peninsula across the bay and one of the only places in the county where you can enjoy views of the Brandon, Slieve Mish and the MacGillycuddy's Reeks mountain ranges from the same location. Take a right at the T-junction for an 8km return journey out towards the pier, along the pebble beach, returning to the church again. Continue straight on, following signposts for Glenbeigh. This road rejoins the main **N70** after another 5km at Caragh Bridge. Take a right-hand turn in the direction of Glenbeigh.

The next 3km of the journey takes us to the scenic village of Glenbeigh, a very popular stop along the Ring of Kerry. Go through the village and follow signposts for Rossbeigh to the right, reaching one of the most famous beaches in Kerry at the 27km mark. It is a good place to stop to enjoy the air and the scenery, but it is the next part of the route where a full appreciation of the view can be had. Continue from Rossbeigh up the first climb of the day towards Droum. This climb is short but maybe not sweet, with a constant tough gradient for approximately 1.5km, but there is a greater reason other than the gradient to dismount: the opportunity to appreciate the views from a height back over Rossbeigh and its hinterlands. From the top of this climb the road descends to the main **N70** again. Turn left and head back to Glenbeigh, reaching the village at the 35km mark, which is a good halfway point and opportunity to take a food stop and a much-needed rest.

After refuelling, head back in the direction of Killorglin, passing again the narrow Caragh Bridge after which there is a very slight ascent. Turn right at the signpost for Glencar and Caragh Lake. Shortly afterwards, take the next right-hand turn, signposted for Glencar. The next 8km of this

Alongside the magnificent Caragh Lake.

route will see a gradual ascent alongside the majestic Caragh Lake on a well-surfaced and quiet road that is normally the reserve of locals and the most curious of tourists, as this is slightly off of the main Ring of Kerry road. As soon as the lake is no longer in sight you know that you are entering Glencar. This area is famous for hiking, unsurprisingly, with miles of forest and bog trails available to explore. At approximately the 54km mark follow the signpost to the right for the Climbers' Inn, a well-known B&B and bar that serves tea and coffee and is a great spot to stop and appreciate the natural beauty that this part of Kerry has to offer.

Leave the Climbers' Inn heading north-eastwards back to Killorglin for the final section of the route. The next 3km stretch is on a steady gradual ascent that rises up towards the freshwater lake, Lough Acoose. From here, the remainder of the journey is downhill with Killorglin in the distance and spectacular views of its surrounds, visible for most of the way. Continue until you meet a T-junction, where you turn left, back into Killorglin town. You have two options for the return to the car. At the crossroads in Killorglin you can turn left up the main street on a short climb, famous in the county for being part of the final stage of the annual Rás Mumhan on Easter weekend, and then turn right at the top of the hill back to the church; alternatively, go straight ahead, which will lead you directly back to the car park opposite the church where the journey began.

Glencar and Caragh Bridge.

19. Sliabh Luachra Loop

Rathmore – Knocknagree – Ballydesmond – Scartaglen –
Castleisland – Currow – Kilsarcon – Barraduff – Rathmore

A hilly, rural cycle in an area rich in music and heritage.

Grade: 4   **Height gain:** 885m

Distance: 80km   **Time:** 3½ to 4½ hours

Climbs:

Category	Length	Start/End Points	Start/End Elevation	Average Gradient
5	4km	1km / 5km	132m / 196m	1.6%
4	3km	12km / 15km	190m / 281m	4%
3	7km	28.5km / 35.5km	71m / 274m	3%
5	2km	40km / 42km	148m / 200m	3%
5	2km	43.5km / 45.5km	167m / 214m	2%

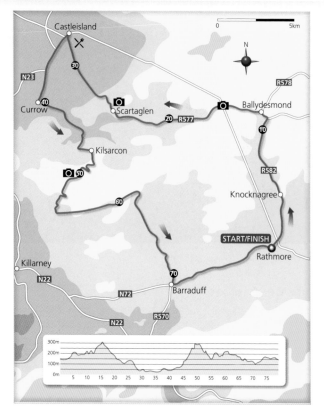

Start/Finish

This route begins in the east Kerry town of Rathmore, just 20km outside Killarney. There is usually plenty of parking available within the town. A useful spot for parking is near the Centra/Topaz filling station, which is just on the eastern side of the town.

Sliabh Luachra, with a name that roughly translates as 'Mountain of Rushes', encompasses parts of Kerry, Cork and Limerick that are synonymous with music and the arts. This route aims to take you on a heritage-laden journey through several of the towns within the region and includes some fantastic climbing as well as pacey, rolling roads. You never know: you just might get the opportunity to hear some traditional music in the style unique to this region while passing by the many pubs along the way.

In Kilsarcon, looking east towards Scartaglen.

Route description

Leave Rathmore and take the **R582**, signposted for Knocknagree and Ballydesmond, briefly heading across the county border into Cork and reaching the quaint village of Knocknagree after only after 5km and Ballydesmond after 12km. Knocknagree punches way above its weight in terms of its heritage and, as well as being famous for its music, it

The ascent of Bawnaglanna between Scartaglen and Kilcummin.

was also where the famous eighteenth-century poet Eoghan Ruadh Ó Súilleabháin died. The road from Rathmore to Ballydesmond is quite rolling with a number of small ascents, which are just enough to warm up the legs for the road ahead. Just before Ballydesmond you will reach a T-junction where you turn left onto the **R577** and back into County Kerry. From here, the road rises again for a category 4 climb but it is relatively short, at just 3km. At the summit of this climb is a crossroads in an area known as Knocknaboul, with impressive panoramic views. From here, continue straight on for a nice, lively descent towards Scartaglen. Just after this crossroads there is a commemorative plaque on the left-hand side, marking the site of the ambush at Tureengarbh Glen, which took place in January 1921 during the War of Independence.

The descent continues on from here until the road levels; a small rise will bring you into the village of Scartaglen with 25km completed. Scartaglen, 'Where the women chase the men …' as the locals cheerfully say, has a rich heritage of music, dancing and drama and hosts many events in its 200-seater heritage and arts centre. Continue from here along the **R577** where another lively descent and rolling road will bring you into the town of Castleisland, home of the annual Padraig O'Keeffe music festival. Here is a good place to stop for tea or coffee and there are plenty of shops and restaurants in the town.

From Castleisland, take the **N28** towards Killarney briefly, until the 35km mark where our route turns left, following signposts for Currow. Take a left-hand turn in Currow at the church and a subsequent right at a fork in the road after another 2km. This takes you over a bridge and on to a T-junction, where you turn left, following signs briefly towards Scartaglen again. At the 44km mark turn right, following the signpost for Kilsarcon, and just afterwards at another fork on the road, turn right again, ignoring signs for Kilsarcon Graveyard.

This is the end of complicated directions for a while as the road climbs up towards Bawnaglanna on a road little known for cycling in the county but a spectacular one nonetheless. This stretch is a category 3 climb and is roughly 7km long but in reality the distance is not noticeable as the scenery and pleasure gained from climbing are very distracting as the route loops and winds its way up a scenic valley. The top of this climb, with a mast at the summit, is visible for miles around.

There is a very fast descent after this climb with wonderful views of the Lakes of Killarney ahead on a nice day as we roll on towards a T-junction where we left. This is the parish of Kilcummin; our route, however, does not enter the village itself, instead opting to carry straight on for another 6km until reaching Anablaha School, which is a very distinctive yellow building. Take the right-hand turn just before the school and another right at a T-junction. Around here the countryside changes briefly, leaving behind the fertile landscape for bogland, which has its own charms.

Continue on until you see a signpost for Barraduff to your left. Take this left turn and cycle on, passing a crossroads and reaching Barraduff at the 70km mark. From Barraduff turn left onto the **N72** for the remaining 10km, which is rolling and pacey as it returns you to the starting point in Rathmore.

20. The Dan Paddy Andy Figure of Eight

Maglass – Glanageenty – Dan Paddy Andy crossroads – Listowel – Knocknagoshel – Kielduff – Maglass

Discovering the hidden gems and quiet back roads of north Kerry.

Grade: 4			**Height gain:** 950m	
Distance: 83km			**Time:** 3½ to 4 hours	
Climbs:				
Category	Length	Start/End Points	Start/End Elevation	Average Gradient
3	5.4km	1.2 / 6.6km	48 / 231m	3.3%
4	7.8km	33.5 / 41.3km	31 / 174m	1.8%
5	3.31km	60.4 / 63.9km	157 / 255m	2.8%

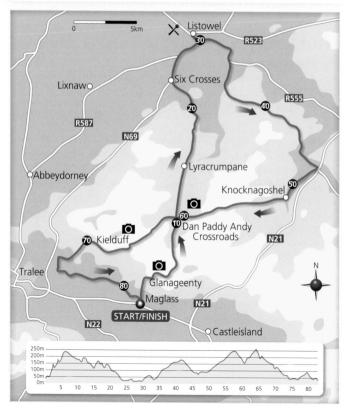

Kilmanihan west.

Start/Finish

From Tralee, take the **N21** in the direction of Castleisland and Limerick. The start point is at O'Riada's Bar in Maglass, Ballymacelligott. This is midway between Tralee and Castleisland. There are spaces for a few cars in close proximity to the bar (at the trailhead for Glannageenty forest trail).

Daniel Patrick Andrew (Dan Paddy Andy) O'Sullivan (1899–1966) was the last of the great Irish matchmakers. The man's name is synonymous with the pronounce-it-if-you-can Lyracrumpane area, as well as the crossroads that this route twice passes through. From the off, this route offers plenty of variety: some short but challenging climbs, an abundance of quiet countryside and peaceful roads that are well hidden from some of the busy highways close by.

Route description

Cycling away from the main road in a northerly direction, take a left turn at the T-junction. After 600m, turn right and follow the small brown signs marked Trailhead, which lead up a narrow road to the right. Almost immediately this modest road kicks up into a pretty steep ascent, which should have all but the very strongest of cyclist reaching for their low gears. Once at the summit, the fun is not quite over as the road continues in an almost rollercoaster fashion, twisting through one or two sharp bends as it passes through the Glanageenty walking trails, an area steeped in folklore and history. Glanageenty comes from the Irish *Gleann na gCaointe*, which roughly translates as 'the Glen of Mourning' and may have taken its name from the fact that the last knighted Earl of Desmond, Gerald FitzGerald, was beheaded in the area in 1583. Also the area was a refuge in 1916 for one of Roger Casement's companions, Robert Monteith, who evaded his enemies here after the unsuccessful arms landing at Banna Strand. These three superb trails are very much the work of the local running legend, John Lenihan, who honed his skills in these very hills. In 1988 John ran up and down Carrauntoohil Mountain (Ireland's highest peak) in 71 minutes 43 seconds, a record that still stands.

Once up a second steep, twisting ascent, take a right turn at the small crossroads (signposted Captain Monteith 1916 Memorial and Glanageenty Woods parking). Go past the main car park before continuing up a hill. The views are dominated by the many species of native Irish trees in the surrounding forest and very soon, as the road continues to climb, you become aware that you are cycling almost in line with the tree canopy. Eventually, the road begins to level as it reaches the Listowel-to-Castleisland road. Turn left at the T-junction and travel northwards, first through bogland and then more forest along a steady descent. Continue through the locally named Dan Paddy Andy or Reanagowan crossroads and up the sharp ascent towards Lyracrumpane. This stretch of rolling road is known as the Listowel Road and continues straight through to the Six Crosses, on the outskirts of Listowel.

Take a right turn at the Six Crosses onto the **N69** and follow the busiest road on the route for 6km into Listowel. The town has plenty of refreshment amenities to satisfy the weary cyclist and, as there is little opportunity further into the ride, this is a good place to stop.

Leaving Listowel, cycle back across the river on the **N69** towards Tralee, turning left onto the **R555** in the direction of Abbeyfeale. The road initially runs close to the River Feale as it pulls up and away from Listowel. After approximately 4km on the **R555** turn right, following the signpost for Castleisland and Cork.

The next 13km of cycling are hard earned on a road that lacks the springy surface that would be welcome at this stage of the ride. Turn right at the yellow Westering Inn; after 1.6km follow the road as it branches off to the right for Knocknagoshel; proceed over the River Owveg and be sure to take the left fork in the road. This section of road bypasses the actual village of Knocknagoshel as it rises slowly past the local Gaelic Football grounds. Gradually the fertile agricultural land gives way to bog and heathland as the seemingly endless ascents finally peter out, allowing a welcome descent to the Dan Paddy Andy crossroads. Proceed straight through this intersection, this time travelling west towards Tralee. Proceed up the steady climb through a forested area and towards a summit that

Ascending from Glanageenty onto Bateman's Green, in the direction of the Listowel road.

offers stunning views of the shimmering blue Tralee Bay with the outline of Tralee town visible at the foot of the slopes of Slieve Mish.

The descent towards Tralee is routine and welcome. The road surface is acceptable and the gradient steady. The landscape is open with little protection, but when the sun shines this hardly matters. As the route starts to level out, the road zips through Kielduff, a small townland with a prominent creamery close to the road. Keep an eye out for the old phone box to the left, tastefully decorated with colourful flowers by caring locals.

As the road closes in on Tralee, take a left turn, 3.7km after Kielduff. This hidden turn lies directly after a farm on the left. (If you reach the main roundabout, you have gone too far.) Follow the narrow link road to the next junction. Take a left turn and continue eastwards on this undulating thoroughfare for 8km. On entering Clogher village, keep to the left. Things should start getting familiar as the lane towards the Glanageenty trailhead is passed to the left. The road towards O'Riada's Bar and the starting point is the next turn on the right.

21. The Conor Pass Circuit

Blennerville – Conor Pass – Dingle – Annascaul – Camp – Blennerville

Take the challenge of cycling over one of Ireland's highest passes.

Grade: 5			**Height gain:** 1,201m		
Distance: 89km			**Time:** 4 to 5 hours		
Climbs:					
Category	Length	Start/End Points	Start/End Elevation	Average Gradient	
2	5.1km	31.67km / 36.77km	54m / 478m	8.3%	
5	4.3km	50.2km / 54.5km	4m / 122m	2.7%	
5	4.3km	61km / 65.3km	26m / 159m	3.0%	
5	5km	67km / 72km	121m / 223m	2.0%	

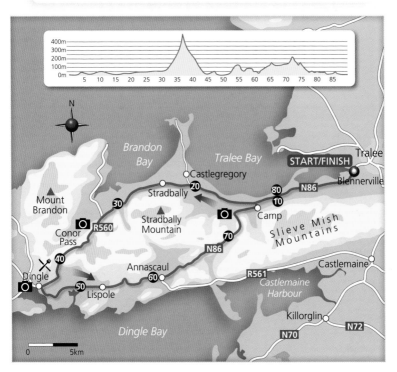

Start/Finish

The route starts in Blennerville (famous for its windmill). The village is a little over 3km from Tralee on the **N86**. The handiest place to park is opposite the windmill in a free car park close to the old railway station.

The Conor Pass is one of Ireland's highest and most spectacular roads. Rising to 478m with a 5km climb from east to west, this is a climb that will live long in the memory. The big bonus after it is completed is the chance to experience Dingle, a vibrant town that gives the visitor that instant 'I'm on holidays' feeling.

Route description

Turn left from the starting point and cycle through Blennerville. Once clear of the village, continue on the fairly straight **N86**, passing through the village of Camp (Lower) and continuing on the **R560** through Stradbally. This road cuts between the coast on the right and the imposing Slieve Mish Mountains to the left. Expect a flat enough ride until the start of the Conor Pass, barring the occasional short hill on the run in to Camp. On passing through Camp (Lower), be sure to follow the signpost for the Conor Pass, which bears right at a fork in the road onto the **R560** and is well signposted.

Once past the Cloghane and Brandon Point junction at 27km the route moves inland towards the Conor Pass itself. The luxuriant landscape is interspersed by the occasional sheep farm, fresh mountain rivers and faraway mountain peaks.

Mount Brandon and the Atlantic Ocean seen from the R560 near Stradbally, cycling in the direction of the Conor Pass.

The view from the top of the Conor Pass.

The approach to the start of the climb remains quite level, with the road signs and the Irish words *Go Mall* (slow) painted on the road surface being the giveaway that something interesting awaits around the corner. As the legs start adjusting to the gradient, the low-lying terrain is a mix of rock and woodland. At about the halfway mark the climb approaches Pedlar's Lake, which is a favourite viewing point for tourists, and the vista opens up to the right, with splendid views of Clogharee Lough and Lough Gal.

Past Pedlar's Lake the climb alters slightly, insomuch as parts of the road seem intertwined with the side of the mountain, leaving small sections of the route very narrow in places and the mountain rock wall within touching distance. Exercise an element of caution in these areas as space is tight. Within striking distance of the summit things open up, but not before the mountain attempts one last kick, until you have the joy of a flat surface once more.

Congratulations! That's the Conor Pass ascent completed. The top of the pass offers fine views of the Maharees, Mount Brandon and the Loop Head peninsula in County Clare, provided the weather is clear. Please note, however, that visibility on the summit can be quite poor on a bad day.

The descent into Dingle is 7km long and a pleasurable experience. Be sure to go carefully, even though the surface of the road is excellent and the bends are gentle. On reaching Dingle, take a right turn up Main Street and then turn left down Green Street, past the church and left onto Bridge Street. This area offers numerous restaurants, cafes, bars and shops. Dingle is well worth a stop, to refuel and reflect on a job well done.

Cycle along Bridge Street and at the roundabout take the second exit, onto the **N86**, which is signposted for Tralee and Killarney and passes the Esso garage to the left. Take the second exit at the next roundabout as the route leading out of Dingle takes on a slight incline, but there is compensation in the splendid views of Dingle Bay down to the right. Once past the Dingle racecourse, the road takes a few twists and turns before dropping down onto a long, straight section, which passes through the village of Lispole. From here on there is a steady climb of 4.3km before a nice downhill stretch towards Annascaul that includes three hairpin bends.

On entering Annascaul, pass the South Pole Inn on the left, the former residence of the explorer Tom Crean. Inside the pub are pictures and artefacts, logging his heroic exploits in the Antarctic. It is also possible to visit his grave by taking a left turn up a narrow road just before the South Pole Inn. The grave lies between the village and secluded Annascaul Lake.

The route out of Annascaul sees the **N86** continue north-eastwards with a steady climb of 10km. Part of the route includes an excellent cycle path. Sadly this lasts for only a few short kilometres before we have to share the main road once again. On reaching the peak of this climb at Gleann na nGealt, be sure to soak up the fine views to the north of Loop Head, Kerry Head, Fenit and the Maharees. This section of the route descends for 6km, passing through Camp (Upper). At the T-junction, turn right back onto the **N86**, following the main road eastwards, towards Blennerville and Tralee and our starting point.

On the approach to Annascaul.

22. Sneem and Kenmare Loop

Torc – Moll's Gap – Sneem – Kenmare – Moll's Gap – Torc

Renowned climbing and scenery galore.

Grade: 4			**Height gain:** 1,243m	
Distance: 90km			**Time:** 4 to 4½ hours	
Climbs:				
Category	Length	Start/End Points	Start/End Elevation	Average Gradient
3	10km	5km / 15km	24m / 270m	1.9%
5	4km	26.5km / 30.5km	49m / 170m	3.1%
3	9km	63km / 72km	20m / 270m	2.3%

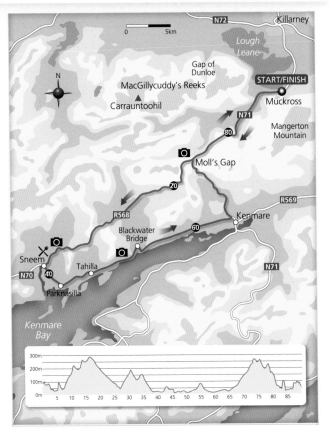

Ladies' View, Killarney.

Start/Finish

The starting point for this route is in Torc Waterfall car park, which is well signposted and located just 5km outside Killarney on the **N71** road to Kenmare.

This route offers a rewarding opportunity to visit Kenmare and Sneem, two very popular and scenic areas on the Ring of Kerry. There are incredible views along the way including Ladies View, the Black Valley and the Beara Peninsula. Like most rewarding things in life, however, there is a little exertion involved, in this case the matter of Moll's Gap, which is the gatekeeper for both the outward and return journeys. There are two ascents of the same climb from different approaches, but little in common in terms of views except for the summit.

Route description

Leave Torc Waterfall car park and head south-westwards along the **N71**. For the first few kilometres the road is rolling and fast; however, it will gradually begin to rise for the first ascent of the day towards Moll's Gap. The ascent itself is never too steep, with an average gradient of approximately 2%, but it is relatively long and it will be at the 15km mark before Moll's Gap is reached. Here there is a café that has an impressive upstairs vista of the Black Valley if a quick break is needed. Take a right at the summit, signposted for Sneem (**R568**) past Lough Barfinnihy for a welcome descent for the next 10km, enjoying views of Ballaghbeama Pass to your right and the Blackwater area to your left. There is another climb further on, this time a gradual effort for 4km, before the road descends again, reaching Sneem at the 36km mark.

Sneem, as a village, is well worth a stop as it has a number of cafés and shops but there is also a lovely character about the place that can only be appreciated with a meander around, from the bronze statue of Steve 'The Crusher' Casey, world champion wrestler and a native of the village, to the main bridge, which overlooks the estuary of the River Sneem as it flows towards the Atlantic. Sneem is the best place on this route to take your main food stop of the day.

Leaving Sneem, head eastwards on the **N70** signposted for Kenmare. This road is on the main Ring of Kerry route and is quite well surfaced. A few kilometres outside Sneem is the Parknasilla Hotel, set amidst woodland, inlets and hidden beaches. It was here that the film *The Lobster,* starring Colin Farrell, was shot in 2014. Continue along the **N70**, passing over the Blackwater Bridge, which is almost 200 years old. Further down the road lies the village of Templenoe, home to the Spillane brothers who were famous Gaelic footballers for Kerry in the 1980s. As well as being involved in TV punditry and journalism, Pat Spillane also owns a bar in the village.

You will reach Kenmare after approximately 63km, arriving at a T-junction where the left-hand road will take you back towards Moll's Gap along the **N71**. If you wish to visit Kenmare, take a quick detour to the right. At the meeting point of the Iveragh and Beara peninsulas, Kenmare is a vibrant town with many shops and restaurants. The largest Bronze Age

Heading back to Kenmare from Sneem with views of the Beara Peninsula to the right.

stone circle in the south-west of Ireland is located close to the town. The Brennan brothers, Francis and John, own the five-star Park Hotel in the town as well as starring in the popular TV series *At Your Service*. Feel free to get a bit of food here, but be aware that very soon after leaving the town, the ascent to Moll's Gap begins and it might not feel comfortable to do this on a full stomach; however, something light would be worthwhile.

Leave the T-junction, having taken a left, and almost immediately the second ascent of Moll's Gap of the day will begin. This approach is a little shorter than the one earlier in the day but is more noticeable in terms of gradient, especially at the point when the landscape opens up before you and you can just make out the gap in the distance above. On reaching the summit, having completed 75km, it will be a great reassurance to know that the majority of the day's labours are behind you. Take a moment to stop here and appreciate the views back downs to the Lakes of Killarney, the Black Valley and Muckross, which seem minute in the distance beneath. Leave Moll's Gap and head down towards Killarney, with a pleasant descent awaiting you as you roll down to the car park at Torc Waterfall.

Ascending Moll's Gap from Kenmare.

23. The Three Climbs and Two Counties Cycle

Killarney – Ballyvourney – Coom – Kilgarvan – Kenmare – Killarney

A sneak visit across the county bounds for some excellent climbing and rolling terrain.

Grade: 4

Distance: 100km

Climbs:

Height gain: 1,201m

Time: 4 to 4½ hours

Category	Length	Start/End Points	Start/End Elevation	Average Gradient
3	6km	19.5km / 25.5km	91m / 292m	4%
4	3km	39km / 42km	163m / 290m	4%
3	9km	66.5km / 75.5km	20m / 270m	2.3%

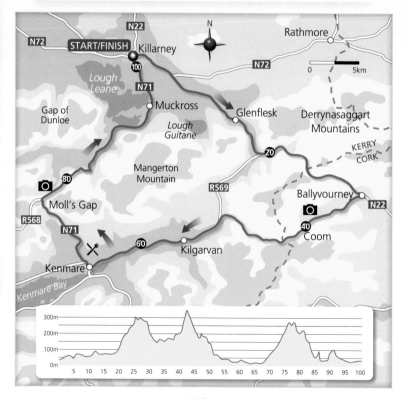

Start/Finish

The route starts in the public car park near St Mary's Cathedral on the **R877** in Killarney. Approaching Killarney from the **N72**, follow signs for Kenmare and the town centre at the Ballydowney Roundabout. Turn left just after the cathedral and find the car park situated off to the left.

The gradual ascent towards Coom from Ballyvourney.

This route offers spectacular scenery on roads that take you for a quick detour into County Cork. It includes three challenging climbs, each with their own scenic rewards, culminating in a stunning descent back down towards Killarney that will whet the appetite for a return visit.

Route description

Leaving the car park, head north along the **R877** towards the Ballydowney Roundabout and take the second exit onto the **N72**. There are another two roundabouts in quick succession after this: be sure to follow signposts for Cork at each one to reach the main Killarney-to-Cork road and the first part of your cycle. This stretch of road is well surfaced and, although probably busy with traffic, it has a hard shoulder for most of the way to Ballyvourney which allows the chance to enjoy the changing landscape as you leave Killarney and head for the county boundary with Cork. It is on the approach to the county border that the first climb of the day appears with a steady drag all the way past the *Capall Mór* – an imposing O'Donoghue-Ross statue of a horse standing high above the road – to the 'Welcome to Cork' sign, but this foray into the Rebel County is short-lived, at least for today.

The descent from the county bounds is a welcome respite from the previous climb and continues quickly as the road narrows and approaches Ballyvourney. Before entering the village and shortly after the Mills Inn bar and restaurant, turn right following signposts for Kenmare and Coolea. From here, the road narrows slightly but the hustle and bustle of the traffic should now be behind you. Soon you will enter the charming village of Coolea and the heart of the Gaeltacht. Continue straight through the village towards the second climb of the day, at Coom. This ascent begins almost meagrely but ends with a flourish and boasts beautiful views of the rugged Roughty Valley that separates the two counties. The top of Coom is marked by Creedon's bar, arguably the highest pub in Ireland, a claim contested by Johnny Fox's pub in Dublin. A quick, winding descent down through the valley takes you back into County Kerry and on to Morley's Bridge and a T-junction onto the **R569**. Turn left here towards Kilgarvan on some of the best-maintained roads in Ireland. Maybe it has something to do with some famous local politicians? Carry on through Kilgarvan on some very rolling roads for another 10km reaching Kenmare with 65km completed so far.

At the intersection between the Iveragh and Beara Peninsulas, Kenmare is well placed as a bustling market town and tourism centre and offers many shops and restaurants for a food stop and quick browse, if desired.

When you are ready to set off again, head straight through the town in a north-westerly direction on the **N71**, following signposts for Killarney. The last climb of the day awaits and it is the noteworthy Moll's Gap, famous

Creedon's Pub at the top of Coom, Ireland's highest pub.

as the last climb of the charity Ring of Kerry Cycle every year and normally the first question people hear when they get back to Killarney, 'How did you find Moll's?'

The climb begins almost immediately upon leaving Kenmare and kicks off very gradually. The first half of the climb is hidden and well sheltered; however, as the landscape opens up about a third of the way up a better appreciation for the effort ahead can be realised. The ascent itself has some alpine qualities with some imposing rock faces and a few switchback bends, but the landscape is unmistakably Kerry. Upon reaching the top of Moll's Gap at the 75km mark, you will find a café and toilet facilities, if needed; there is plenty of room to stop for a moment to appreciate the views of the Black Valley and Lakes of Killarney beneath.

Set off once more along the **N71** towards Killarney, on what is one of the most scenic descents in Kerry, passing the entrances to Torc Waterfall, Muckross House and Gardens, and reaching Killarney after 96km. Upon entering Killarney keep left and follow signposts for Killorglin and Tralee until reaching the end of the Mission Road. Here is the cathedral and the car park where the day's journey began.

The top of Moll's Gap before a welcome descent back to Killarney.

24. North Kerry and the Coast Road

Listowel – Ballybunion – Tarbert – Glin – Athea – Abbeyfeale – Listowel

A great opportunity to explore the beauty of the north Kerry coastline, away from the busiest tourist traps.

Grade: 4

Height gain: 870m

Distance: 100km

Time: 4½ to 5 hours

Climbs:

Category	Length	Start/End Points	Start/End Elevation	Average Gradient
4	8.5km	51.5km / 60km	5m / 166m	2%
4	4.5km	66km / 70.5km	62m / 204m	3.2%
5	2.5km	84.5km / 87km	66m / 110m	1.9%

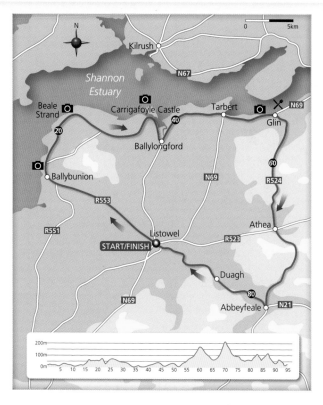

The Blue Flag 'Ladies Beach' in Ballybunion.

Start/Finish

This route begins in Listowel, 30km north of Tralee, where there are several opportunities for parking including a convenient location just off Convent Street in the town centre where there is a large car park near the SuperValu shop.

The roads along the coastline of north Kerry have a charm that would rival any other scenery in the country, as the landscape changes from golden beaches to windswept heath to rich agricultural land. Where better to start and conclude this adventure than in the culture-rich heritage town of Listowel, home of the famous playwright John B. Keane? With many towns and villages en route this cycle seems to fly by, with each landmark telling a different and intriguing story.

Route description

Follow signposts in the town centre for Ballybunion, leading on past Convent Street. Follow the **R553**, which is mostly flat and perfect for warming up the legs. After 15km pass through Lisselton, before arriving in Ballybunion a further 7km on. This seaside town is renowned for its picturesque beach and championship golf course, played by President Bill Clinton in 1998. Continuing through the town and cycle northwards onto the **R551**, following signs for the Wild Atlantic Way, which lead to a gentle climb out of Ballybunion. Take a left turn 1km after leaving the town, signposted for Beale Strand. This area boasts over 3km of beaches and dunes as well as magnificent views across the Shannon Estuary to

County Clare, with Kilrush visible on the clearest of days. Continue along this undulating road until it merges with the **R551** again, taking a left turn, signposted for Asdee.

After passing through Asdee, the road continues eastwards in the direction of Ballylongford. At 3km outside Asdee, turn left upon meeting a signpost signalling 4km to Ballylongford and proceed down the narrow road. This road is part of a looped detour towards Carrig Island and the single-tower fifteenth-century castle at Carrigafoyle, one of the strongholds of the Earl of Desmond until it was besieged by Cromwellian forces in 1580. Enough still stands of the castle to merit the name it is still called, 'The Guardian of the Shannon'. Be aware that this road is rough in parts and floods on occasion. Beyond the castle the route enters the village of Ballylongford at the 37km mark.

Take a left turn back onto the **R551** and proceed for another 10km along a flat stretch of road until reaching Tarbert. The town is well known for its ferry to Killimer in County Clare. There is a 4km detour along the banks of the River Shannon to visit the ferry terminal, to avail of the views, the bar and toilet facilities there. Leaving Tarbert, continue along **N69** coast road that enters quickly into County Limerick and the heritage town of Glin. Glin has a colourful past and is steeped in medieval history. The Fitzgerald

Carrigafoyle Castle outside Ballylongford, beside the River Shannon.

Statue of the playwright and author John B. Keane in Listowel.

castle, built around 1200, is still visible, with the later castle, built around 1780, impressively dominating the surroundings. The village has a number of shops and cafés and is a good place to refuel.

Take a right turn and follow signposts for Athea on the **R524** along a road that has a surprisingly difficult incline from the outset. Along here, the landscape changes to heath and woodland as the route heads inland and upwards with a leg-testing climb of approximately 8km in length, after which there is a swift descent into Athea with 72km completed so far. If tempted (and tired), it is possible at Athea to follow signposts for Listowel for an optional shortcut back to the start; however, for those with remaining energy and resolve, follow the signposts through Athea for Abbeyfeale. A 3.5km climb out of Athea is followed by a steady 8km descent into Abbeyfeale.

On entering Abbeyfeale turn right onto the **R555**, signposted for Listowel. The brief sojourn in County Limerick comes to an end as the route crosses over the River Feale and enters back into County Kerry. This final stretch of road has a number of small climbs, with the standout hill being in the village of Duagh, but overall there is nothing too taxing. Continue north-eastwards beside the River Feale until the road merges with the **N69**. Take a right turn and cycle over the impressive five-arch bridge traversing the River Feale back into Listowel and receive a friendly wave from the statue of John B. Keane in the town centre, welcoming you back after a very satisfying journey.

25. Kenmare and Coom

Kenmare – Glengarriff – Ballylickey – Ballingeary – Top of Coom – Kenmare

This is a classic route that includes two counties, two passes, spectacular sea and mountain views on reasonably quiet roads.

Grade: 4/5   **Height gain:** 1,344m

Distance: 100km   **Time:** 4½ to 5½ hours

Climbs:

Category	Length	Start/End Points	Start/End Elevation	Average Gradient
2	7km	11.3km / 18.3km	76m / 330m	3.6%
5	3km	28km / 31.0km	4m / 88m	2.2%
2	10km	45.5km / 55.5km	32m / 224m	1.9%
3	8km	62.4km / 70.4km	89m / 366m	3.4%
5	2km	73.8km / 75.8km	244m / 345m	5%

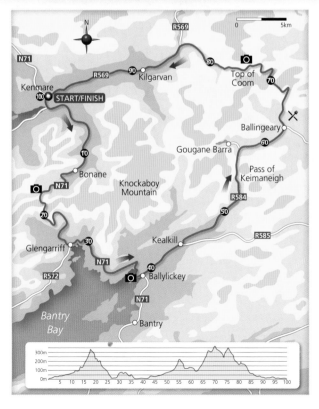

Start/Finish

This route begins in Kenmare where parking should not be a difficulty within the town itself. There is a public car park opposite Kenmare Holy Cross church just off of the main square. There are also toilet facilities adjacent to the car park.

Starting in the south Kerry market town of Kenmare, this route takes in the scenic Caha Pass and its unique tunnels before entering County Cork. Descend into the village of Glengarriff and its many natural attractions before cycling along the pristine **N71** road towards west Cork.

Moving inland, tackle the Pass of Keimaneigh, before visiting Ballingeary and taking on the hilly Coom. Cross back over the border to County Kerry and pass by Ireland's highest pub.

This is a challenging route on moderately quiet roads, which will be a joy for anyone who considers themselves anything from an average to experienced cyclist.

The Caha Pass tunnels.

116

Route description

From Kenmare's main square follow the one-way system onto Main Street. Take the second exit at the roundabout adjacent to the Lansdowne Arms hotel. Continue on the **N71**. At the end of the street bear left at the post office and cycle over the bridge. Go south on the **N71**, following signs for Skibbereen and Glengarriff.

Once over Our Lady's Bridge, the route leads up a gentle ascent of 11km, passing through the small village of Bonane, after which the main climb starts, before reaching the summit of the Caha Pass and the Kerry/Cork border. For much of the first 10km the terrain is verdant, with the sound of streams and waterfalls being prominent. At Bonane, the landscape starts to open up, with spectacular views of the Sheen Valley and Priest's Leap area to the left.

Bonane is well known for its Heritage Park, which contains various artefacts of ancient Irish history and archaeology. Within the area are several walking trails, and it is also a significant dark-sky viewing area for stargazers.

Once past Bonane, the road widens slightly and offers an excellent surface. The climb to the top of the Caha Pass is quite unique, with small tunnels dotting the route to the summit. At the top, admire the fine views and review the road to the top of the pass, as it is quite easy to identify in the valley below.

Go through the final tunnel and into County Cork. The descent is 9km into Glengarriff. The views from the top at the Cork side are well worth taking in, with the spectacular Bantry Bay being the most prominent sight. As the road descends into Glengarriff, the rugged mountain landscape gives way to a subtropical profusion of flora, with colourful flowers adorning the roadside.

On reaching Glengarriff, bear slightly to the left, but remain with the **N71**. Follow the road through the village, with the idyllic Glengarriff Harbour to the right. Continue on up the hill and away from the village in the direction of Bantry. The road climbs steadily for 3km, passing alongside stunning properties, the local golf club and the Bamboo Park! This section of the route is arguably one of the best road surfaces in the country, making this segment a joy as you ride along the sweeping Bantry Bay coastline. The views of Whiddy Island and the Sheep's Head Peninsula just enhance the experience.

Continuing on to the village of Ballylickey, take a left turn onto the **R584**, signposted for Macroom. This turning is on an awkward bend, so stay alert!

The route starts to move inland in a north-easterly direction. We quickly exchange the coast for an agricultural environment interspersed by small villages. Stay with the **N584** through Kealkill. The majority of this section is

The Pass of Keimaneigh.

of a rolling nature with an overall ascent. The most demanding part comes approximately 10km before Ballingeary. This is the Pass of Keimaneigh. As mountain passes go, it is quite straightforward. The climb to the top is more of a steady pull than anything too steep. The 8km descent into Ballingeary is more than welcome, as it is the first downhill break since Ballylickey. On approaching Ballingeary, the road nears the lake and the early Christian church at Gougane Barra, which lies at the end of a minor road just to the west. The approach into the village is very attractive as the road runs alongside the twisting River Lee.

On entering Ballingeary the road crosses the river. Ballingeary is a good place to take a break. The village has a few pubs and shops to choose from. Once refuelled, proceed for almost 1km through the village before turning left onto the **L3402**. This road is signposted for Ballyvourney (*Baile Bhúirne*). Bear in mind is that this area is Irish (Gaelic) speaking, and so all of the signage is in Irish. As the route leaves Ballingeary, there is a challenging 5km ascent to the beginning of the Coom road. The climb is in quite a rugged area that is a mixture of bogland and bare mountain.

The left-hand turn at the top of the road is quite easy to identify as a big sign points the way to the 'Top of the Coom'. The other road signage was in need of repair at the time of writing, but points to Kenmare and Kilgarvan. Initially, this stretch takes a few minutes to adjust to, as it is decidedly narrow compared to the previous roads, as well as being a little rough for the first kilometre. The first section hugs the side of the mountain in an exciting, twisting fashion, before descending steadily towards a wooded area and then ascending to meet the top of Coom. You are now back in County Kerry, and cannot fail to miss Ireland's highest pub, Creedon's, well signed as The Top of Coom. There has been a friendly rivalry going for many years with Johnnie Fox's in Glencullen, County Dublin, as to which of them the accolade belongs. A letter on the pub wall from the Ordnance Survey Office appears to resolve the issue in favour of Creedon's.

This section of the route is extremely quiet, underlining the need for cyclists and adventurers to be somewhat self-sufficient. Carrying ample sustenance and the right kit in case of a mechanical breakdown should see anyone through this 16km cycle safely.

After an exhilarating descent from the top of Coom, the route finally joins up with the **R695** at Morley's Bridge. Take a left turn at the T-junction and within 4.5km the road enters Kilgarvan, home to a well-known Irish political family, the Healy-Raes. The area around here is very rural, with farming providing the main income. The locality is quite appealing, with the previous rugged landscape giving way to rich pasture. The final 10km leads into Kenmare. The road is in excellent condition and is not too hard on the legs, with some gentle inclines being the final test of your stamina.

Once in Kenmare, follow the **R695** onto the **N71** and take the first exit at the roundabout in front of the Lansdowne Hotel. At the end of Shelbourne Street turn right at the post office onto Henry Street, following the road to the centre of the town and the square.

The Top of Coom.

26. Mini Ring of Kerry

Glencar – Ballaghisheen Pass – Waterville – Sneem –
Blackwater Bridge – Ballaghbeama Pass – Glencar

Some difficult climbing amidst remarkable terrain.

Grade: 5

Distance: 104km

Height gain: 1,358m

Time: 4½ to 5½ hours

Climbs:

Category	Length	Start/End Points	Start/End Elevation	Average Gradient
3	6.2km	1.6km / 7.8km	45m / 278m	4%
3	5.7km	31.5km / 37.2km	6m / 207m	3%
4	2.2km	57.8km / 60km	11m / 117m	4%
3	4.2km	89.3km / 93.5km	50m / 275m	5%

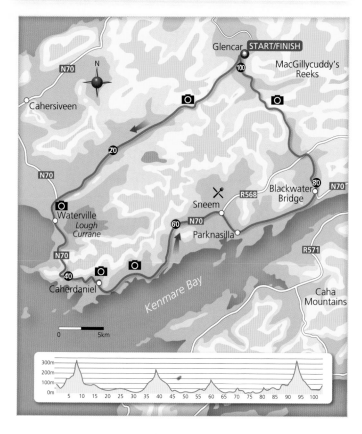

Start/Finish

This route begins at the Climbers' Inn, a well-known B&B and bar in Glencar in the heart of the Iveragh Peninsula. It is situated just under 16km south-west of Killorglin and best accessed by taking the Annadale Road for a kilometre from Killorglin town centre, and then taking a right turn, following signposts for Glencar. Continue along this road until reaching the well-signposted Climbers' Inn, where there is ample parking on the opposite side of the road.

This cycle is the baby brother of the popular Ring of Kerry route but in distance only. It travels on a hilly 104km loop that joins with the main **N70** Wild Atlantic Way route from Waterville to Blackwater Bridge, before cutting through the Iveragh Peninsula onto peaceful country roads away from tourist traffic. This route also incorporates some famous climbs including Ballaghisheen, Coomakista and Ballaghbeama, each climb notorious or praiseworthy, depending on who you ask. The summit of each of these climbs offers a different and unique landscape that, combined, will leave you with a great appreciation for the beauty that this unspoiled region has to offer.

Route description

Begin from the Climbers' Inn and head south-westwards with a view of Ballaghisheen Pass ahead in the distance. The first couple of kilometres of this cycle are very forgiving as the road feels pacey underneath a bicycle and pair of legs that are still warming up. Only shortly afterwards, however, those distant mountains begin to

A signpost for the first challenging climb of the day at Ballaghisheen Pass.

draw you in as the road gradually begins the ascent of Ballaghisheen. This climb has two personalities: the first 3km are a steady 3% gradient and although the road feels heavy underneath, it is very manageable. The second half of the climb is significantly more demanding and has an average gradient of 9% for approximately 2km, leaving you undoubtedly breathless at a hard climb so soon into the beginning of a cycle but, on the other hand, it is very difficult to find a better way to warm up. At the summit of

Ballaghisheen the view ahead opens up towards the south-westerly tip of the Iveragh Peninsula. The rapid 5km descent rolls on towards the tranquil village of Dromid and eventually, with the aid of the road signs, to Waterville by the sea. This section of the route leads out onto New Chapel Cross at a T-junction. Take the left-hand turn towards Waterville onto the **N70** with 30km of the cycle completed so far.

The next section of the route follows the main **N70** Ring of Kerry and Wild Atlantic Way, arriving at Waterville, famous for its connections with Charlie Chaplin and GAA footballer Mick O'Dwyer, but deservedly famous

Taking a breather at the top of Coomakista to enjoy stunning coastline views.

in its own right for its seafront location, with promenade walks and Atlantic views popular with tourists all year round. The village has a number of shops and cafés and is a good opportunity for a quick refuel.

After Waterville comes the second major climb of the day. Coomakista is not an overly taxing climb, with a steady gradient of 3%. However, it is quite long, at 5.7km, which can lead to a challenging ascent on a blustery day. The scenery at the top of Coomakista is arguably among the best of the entire Ring of Kerry route, with stunning coastal views of O'Carroll's Cove and Derrynane to the fore and Waterville and Ballinskelligs Bay behind.

Travel on from the top of Coomakista and wind your way downwards on a well-surfaced road through Caherdaniel and on to Castlecove. After Castlecove, the road begins to feel a little more difficult to travel with a false flat and eventual rise to the top of Crowley's Height. The statistics show the climb to Crowley's Height between Castlecove and Sneem to be 2.2km but in retrospect it feels somewhat longer. The pacey descent towards Sneem is a nice reward on now having 66km completed. Sneem is a beautiful village that is divided in two by a river of the same name. It is famous along the Ring of Kerry route for its rural character and is a great hub for many attractions to visit nearby such as Staigue Fort, an impressive ring fort said to date from the Iron Age. It is also an ideal location to refuel and recharge before the road ahead.

After Sneem continue along the main **N70** road, following signposts for Kenmare and passing the entrance to the renowned Parknasilla Hotel and Resort before arriving at Blackwater Bridge at the 78km mark. The bridge is easily identifiable with myriad signposts as the route crosses the bridge and takes an immediate left, following directions for Ballaghbeama Pass and Derreendarragh. Shortly afterwards, take the next right at a fork in the road.

The next 6km or so take us through Blackwater on a quiet country road that has a number of small rises and falls and eventually leads to a T-junction on the **R568**. Turn left and shortly afterwards another right, continuing to follow signs for Ballaghbeama Pass. Ahead lies the final climb of the day, but before that there are a number of kilometres of undulating road.

The climb up to Ballaghbeama begins in earnest at the 89km mark and has a very similar approach to the first climb of the day, with a gentle first half and a very testing latter half. The final kilometre of Ballaghbeama averages at over 10% gradient and will really test legs already wearied by previous efforts. Grind up towards a rocky summit as best you can where a sign denoting the top will welcome you, no doubt a sight for sore eyes and legs at this point.

There are approximately 10km left on this route, which happily does not include any more climbing, with a lively descent and rolling road guiding you on to a T-junction. Turn right onto a familiar road towards Glencar, with only 1km more to the starting point.

The very smooth tarmacked surface on the approach to Ballaghbeama.

123

27. The Ring of Beara

*Kenmare – Lauragh – Eyeries – Allihies – Castletownbere –
Adrigole – Glengarriff – Kenmare*

A tough but beautiful loop of a rugged peninsula with
unrivalled scenery – a classic!

Grade: 5   **Height gain:** 1,485m

Distance: 140km   **Time:** 6 to 7 hours

Climbs:

Category	Length	Start/End Points	Start/End Elevation	Average Gradient
5	4.8km	48.4km / 53.2km	10m / 80m	1.5%
4	1.1km	62.9km / 64km	20m / 121m	8%
4	5.5km	66.5km / 71.5km	8m / 129m	2.3%
5	5.5km	99km / 104.5km	13m / 118m	1.9%
3	8km	112km / 120km	2m / 270m	4%

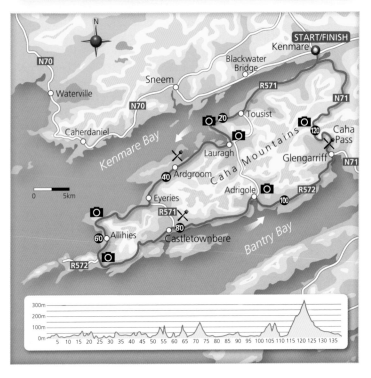

Kilmacalogue Pier, Lauragh.

Start/Finish

This route begins in Kenmare where parking should not be a difficulty within the town. There is a public car park opposite Kenmare Holy Cross church just off of the main square. There are also toilet facilities adjacent to the car park.

Although some 30km shorter than the more popular Ring of Kerry, the neighbouring Beara Peninsula has a lot to offer from a cycling and touring point of view, taking visitors along scenery both wild and ancient and through towns that have a charm and authenticity. The coastal roads that surround the peninsula are quiet from a traffic point of view and a lot more peaceful than other areas, giving ample opportunity to enjoy Atlantic views of the Iveragh Peninsula to the north and the Sheep's Head Peninsula and Bere and Whiddy Islands to the south. The terrain along the route is as varied as you would expect for this distance with some challenging climbs, fast descents and everything in between. The beauty and wildness of this region is one to be treasured.

Route description

Begin your Beara adventure by leaving Kenmare and heading south on the **N71** over the bridge across Kenmare Bay. Turn right just after the

The difficult climb at Reentrusk before Allihies.

bridge onto the **R571**, following signposts for Castletownbere. The first 17km or so of this cycle are on rolling roads that cut through forest land with sporadic views of Kenmare Bay and carry you along a very gentle introduction to the day ahead. After 17.5km follow a signpost to the right for Tousist along the **R573** to continue this coastal exploration. As the winding road closely hugs the coastline, keep an eye out for Kilmacalogue Harbour along the way, which has breathtaking ocean views. Continue onwards and rejoin the **R571** at the 29km mark by taking a right-hand turn and heading towards Castletownbere.

One of the most picturesque parts of the cycle – the Lauragh area – lies ahead, with Glanmore Lake worthy of a stop for photographs. The next section of road brings you across the county border into Cork and on to the tranquil villages of Ardgroom and, 7km further, Eyeries, either of which is a great location for a quick food stop. Just after Eyeries follow the signpost for Allihies to the right on the **R575** at the 46km mark. Up until now the roads have been relatively level but that noticeably changes after this turnoff, with several steady but sharp ascents as the road continues to follow the coastline to Allihies. One climb in particular, identifiable by the sudden lack of any easy gear, might require a dismount and brief walk but it is short-lived. The charming old copper-mining village of Allihies is a welcome sight ahead, with a total of 60km completed so far.

The next section of the route brings you along the **R575** and **R572** around the tip of the peninsula on roads that are challenging, with the occasional reprieve of a number of descents. The reward, as the route veers eastwards for the first time, are fine views of Sheep's Head and Bere Island as you travel towards Castletownbere, seventeenth-century home of the O'Sullivan Beare, and Second World War hero, Dr Aidan MacCarthy of MacCarthy's Bar, and presently home to some lovely shops and cafés for some much-needed respite. You are now over halfway, with 80km completed.

Leaving Castletownbere, continue eastwards along the **R572** towards Adrigole on mostly flat terrain. After Adrigole the road again takes on a different characteristic as it widens and rises before a very fast sweeping descent into Glengarriff at the 115km mark. Glengarriff is a very picturesque village and worthy of a quick stop to refuel. Do not eat too much, however, as the next part of the route is the ascent of the Caha Pass, which starts immediately after leaving Glengarriff on the **N71**, making sure to follow signposts for Kenmare. The ascent of the Caha Pass is nowhere near as steep as some of the day's previous climbs, particularly around Allihies, but by now tiredness will inevitably have set in and adequate pacing is recommended; the climb is quite long: just shy of 10km of some scenic ascending lies ahead. At the summit of the Caha Pass is a tunnel, marking your arrival back in County Kerry.

From here the road descends rapidly along the Sheen Valley where there are several areas to stop along the way to enjoy the views, including Molly Gallivan's, a 200-year-old cottage, where the views of the valley and the village of Bonane up ahead are spectacular. In Bonane there is an award-winning chocolatier called Lorge directly across from the church, where one or two tasty truffles might help you along the remaining few kilometres back to Kenmare. From Bonane the road levels and remains flat for the rest of the journey, reaching Kenmare with 140km completed. With lots of highly rated restaurants in the town, what better way to end the day than with some good food and some great memories of a route that will linger on the palate for a long time?

Heading for the tunnel and back into County Kerry at the top of the Caha Pass.

28. The Ring of Kerry

*Killarney – Kenmare – Sneem – Waterville – Cahersiveen
– Killorglin – Killarney*

Arguably the best-known route in Kerry, and with good reason.

Grade: 5
Height gain: 1,741m
Distance: 170km
Time: 7½ to 9 hours

Climbs:

Category	Length	Start/End Points	Start/End Elevation	Average Gradient
4	6.91km	33.7km / 40.6km	24m / 129m	1.5%
5	2.5km	46.25km / 48.7km	61m / 114m	2.1%
3	6.81km	75.5km / 82.3km	5m / 205m	2.9%
4	8.51km	95.2km / 103.7km	11m / 117m	1.2%
3	10.1km	135.2km / 145km	20m / 251m	2.3%
5	2.8km	156.3km / 159km	24m / 88m	2.3%

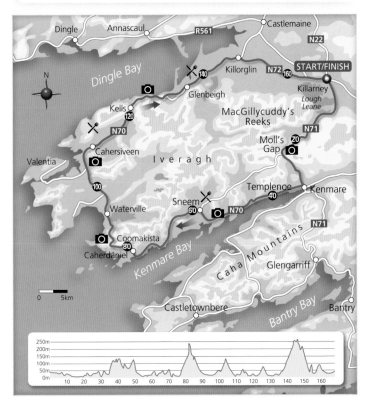

Start/Finish

It can be difficult to find parking in Killarney, especially in summer. A handy place, however, is on the **N71** Muckross Road just beyond the town centre at the start of the Killarney National Park. Pass the INEC to the left and continue for just under 2km. On the left there is a medium-sized car park, which is shared by jarvey carriage men and their horses. Parking here is free.

This is possibly the best-known cycling route in Kerry, mainly due to the charity cycle that attracts thousands of cyclists each July to the area. The good news is that the route is open for the other 364 days of the year and can be done over a few days, or the more challenging one-day cycle. It offers varied and picturesque scenery along a route that really comes into its own between Caherdaniel and Waterville, mainly thanks to the Coomakista Pass and the sparkling views of Deenish Island, Waterville and the Derrynane coastline.

Although it is more traditional to attempt this cycle in an anticlockwise direction around the Ring, this route goes the opposite way. The advantages of this include slightly quieter roads, as most of the tourist traffic follows the traditional route, different views and a flatter finish to the route, with the final testing climb coming just beyond the midway point.

Route description

Turn left out of the car park onto the **N71** and cycle into the Killarney National Park. Pass the entrance to Muckross House and then Torc Waterfall, two iconic attractions in the area. The terrain is wooded, with glimpses of the Killarney lakes to the right. This area is renowned for its wildlife. The early morning cyclist might be lucky and catch a glimpse of a Sika deer.

After a relatively flat start, the first climb of the day, towards Ladies View, begins. The name of the area came about from Queen Victoria's visit to Killarney in the nineteenth century. Apparently it was a favourite spot for her ladies-in-waiting. The views are quite spectacular and well worth a few minutes to stop and admire. After Ladies View the road continues to rise until it reaches Looscaunagh Lough, a very dark-coloured lake popular with trout fishermen. From here on the road surface improves significantly as it climbs gently to Moll's Gap. Moll's Gap is recognisable by the café and gift shop at the summit.

Continue on the **N71** towards Kenmare, following a slight turn to the left and through a gap in the mountain. Follow the mountain-road descent for close on 10km into Kenmare; the descent is not overly steep, allowing for a good pace on a sweeping road. On the outskirts of Kenmare, take the right turn onto the **N70**, signposted for Sneem and Cahersiveen. This turning is just before the filling station on the left.

On the Sneem-to-Derrynane road.

This section of the **N70** road runs through the villages of Templenoe and Tahilla before entering Sneem. Although the road runs close to Kenmare Bay, the coastline is mainly hidden from view by vegetation and houses. There are two steady climbs between Kenmare and Sneem, the first rising from Templenoe and descending towards Blackwater Bridge, with the second a little more exposed descending into Parknasilla.

Sneem is one of the prettiest villages on the Ring of Kerry and well worth a break. It has an abundance of pubs, cafés and shops and is a great place to refuel and relax.

On leaving Sneem there is a bit of work to be done, as the road climbs steadily for 8km. The surrounding terrain offers open views towards the ocean and surrounding mountains. Once the initial climb is finished things get decidedly pleasanter; the route takes a steady descent towards Castlecove and Caherdaniel. The eye-catching part of this section is at O'Carroll's Cove, with its tidy beach running close to the road and Mediterranean-style beach bar.

Located in the foothills of the next major climb (Coomakista) is the village of Caherdaniel. A tiny village, it still has all the amenities needed to keep the visitor happy. The home of Daniel O'Connell, the early nineteenth-century politician nicknamed the Liberator, is now a tourist attraction close to the village. It can be reached by taking a left turn off the main road at Caherdaniel and cycling for approximately 1km.

As the route passes though Caherdaniel on the **N70**, the climb to the summit of Coomakista begins. As climbs go, this is a very steady 6km and nowhere near as arduous as local folklore might have you believe. The next 10km are amongst some of the highlights of the cycle. When the weather is good and the views are clear, it's possible to feast your eyes on the many islands and inlets lying just off the coastline at Derrynane down to the left. At the summit of Coomakista, there are exceptional views of the Kenmare River, Abbey Island, Deenish Island and Scariff Island, as well as

Waterville to the north. There's nearly always some activity at the top of the mountain's large car park, with the summit being a popular stopping-off point for the many coaches that frequent the route.

The descent into Waterville is fairly technical, with a few twists and turns in the road. Caution is advised in wet weather as the surface can become slippery.

Once on flat ground, the next port of call is Waterville, synonymous with the ageing Charlie Chaplin who holidayed in the town during the 1950s and local footballing legend Mick O'Dwyer, Ireland's most successful football manager, who guided Kerry to eight All-Ireland Championships between 1974 and 1989. Like most of the towns and villages on the Ring of Kerry, Waterville has its share of pubs, hotels and cafés. The road runs along the seafront in a typical seaside style. On leaving Waterville, the road pulls away from the coast with the scenery becoming more rugged and boggy in nature, with glimpses of mountains on all sides. Cahersiveen is 16km on from Waterville and straddles the **N70** and is typically busy.

The road out of Cahersiveen climbs steadily for close to 10km. Once at the summit there is a 6km descent past Kells Bay, which lies down to the left. The route then sweeps around in an easterly direction following the Atlantic coastline for a short while. Across the bay there are fine views of the Dingle area and Slea Head. The road continues downhill and comes very close to the old railway viaduct, which was on the Killorglin-to-Cahersiveen railway line in the last century. After the viaduct the road pulls up gently, following the ocean once more, before a sweeping and smooth descent into Glenbeigh. The village offers another place for a break. The next 12km to Killorglin are of a more rolling nature with a number of small hills to remind you that the job isn't quite done. The area is still dominated by mountain views that wane the closer the route gets to Killorglin.

In Killorglin, follow the road through the first roundabout onto Mill Road. Follow this road around to the right and down onto New Line Road before sweeping around to the left and over the Laune River Bridge. At the mini-roundabout, take the third exit, the **N72**, in the direction of Killarney.

With just 20km of the route remaining, the **N72** follows the River Laune to the right-hand side most of the way, with views of the river most prominent on leaving Killorglin. Expect a busier section of road that is relatively flat and worn in sections.

On reaching Killarney take the third exit at the Ballydowney Roundabout onto the **R887** Port Road. Continue onto Mission Road and past the International Hotel. Continue around to the **N71**, following signposts for Kenmare, National Park and Muckross House. Continue straight along Muckross Road for the next 3km. The car park is situated on the left.

The Wild Atlantic Way

The Wild Atlantic Way is a route that has been around for many a year, but thanks to a domestic and international marketing campaign from 2014, lots of signage and minor road improvements, Ireland has now acquired a major tourist attraction from the north to the south along its western coastline. The whole route from County Donegal to County Cork is popular in the main with motorcar tourists, although a good few walkers and cyclists have conquered the 2,500km route.

The Kerry section, which we are concentrating on, covers approximately 400km, from the County Limerick border in the northern village of Tarbert to the border with County Cork, just beyond the village of Lauragh on the Beara Peninsula. The route is well signposted with the distinctive white waves or 'w's joined together on a blue background.

The three routes on offer as part of this Wild Atlantic Way adventure differ slightly from other routes in this guide as they are point to point, rather than starting and finishing in the same places. This will need a bit of logistical planning, depending on whether you wish to tackle the three days consecutively or not.

Getting to Tarbert at the beginning of Day 1 should be easily accessible by bus. Timetables are available on www.buseireann.ie. Bus Éireann buses are generally happy to accommodate cyclists and store bikes safely in the luggage compartment during the journey but a conversation with the bus driver upon departure is well advised.

Day 1 ends in Castlegregory, which is a hive of activity in the summer with a number of nice restaurants and shops. There are also various types of B&B, self-catering and campsite accommodation available. A good resource for further details is http://castlegregorykerry.com/

Day 2 ends in the scenic Glenbeigh at the heart of the Iveragh Peninsula, with several options for dining, evening entertainment and accommodation. More information can be found at http://glenbeigh.ie/.

Day 3 concludes in Ardgroom just over the county border in Cork. The village itself is old-worldy with number of options for food. Although there is accommodation in and around the village of Ardgroom, a room for the night might be a bigger challenge than finding somewhere in a larger town. A search on the Internet or a call to either the Cork or Kerry tourist boards is advised. Some details can also be found on www.discoverbeara.com/accomardgroom.html. The village of Eyeries might also be worth looking at for accommodation if supply is limited in Ardgroom. Eyeries is just 7km from Ardgroom.

There is a limited summer bus service from Bus Éireann passing through the village of Ardgroom, as well as various private companies working different routes on the Beara Peninsula. Information can be found on www.eyeries.ie/bus-transport.php, a website from the nearby village of Eyeries, which includes details on transport in and around Ardgroom also.

It is worth noting that much of the accommodation advertised in these areas is seasonal so it is important to ring ahead to secure and confirm bookings. Also a certain degree of self-sufficiency is important on the journey in the case you need assistance, be it mechanical or otherwise. However, it is a good idea to take a mobile phone with you. Mobile coverage should be sufficient for the majority of the journey.

29. The Wild Atlantic Way – Day 1

Tarbert – Ballybunion – Ballyheige – Fenit – Tralee – Camp – Castlegregory

Starting in rustic north Kerry, follow quiet roads with spectacular sea views, passing through Tralee, before finishing Day 1 in the west Kerry village of Castlegregory.

Grade: 4

Height gain: 842m

Distance: 126km

Time: 6 to 7 hours

Climb: No major climbs on this route.

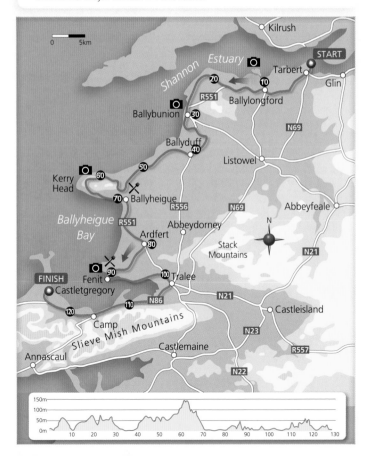

Bromore Cliffs.

Start/Finish

Day 1 begins in Tarbert at the northern tip of the county and the route can be started from either the Tarbert-to-Killimer ferry terminus, or the **N69** Coast Road county bounds with Limerick. This route ends in Castlegregory.

The first day of this Kerry Wild Atlantic Way expedition travels through places seemingly untouched by the twenty-first century, passing by the rugged Bromore Cliffs and through the seaside villages of Ballybunion, Ballyheigue and Fenit, the jaw-droppingly scenic Kerry Head and the county capital of Kerry, Tralee, before passing through Blennerville, the gateway into west Kerry and the Dingle Peninsula, concluding Day 1 at the elegant and welcoming village of Castlegregory.

Route description

The Wild Atlantic Way in north Kerry starts at either the ferry terminus at Tarbert or on the **N69** coast road, where a short section of the route branches off into County Limerick to the village of Foynes, famous for its flying-boat museum.

Exit Tarbert via the **R551**, signposted for Ballybunion, cycling in a south-westerly direction. Initially there is a steady climb out of Tarbert in an area dominated by agriculture and a scattering of roadside shrubs and trees. The road takes on a nice steady 5km ascent into the next village Ballylongford, famed for its summer oyster festival.

Looking across from Kerry Head to the Dingle Peninsula.

Wild Atlantic Way detour – Carrigafoyle Castle

Situated on the banks of the River Shannon estuary and a 5km return trip from Ballylongford is the sixteenth-century Carrigafoyle Castle. Still very much a substantial structure, the 'Guardian of the Shannon', as it has become known, saw its most prominent action in the 1580 Siege of Carrigafoyle Castle. The castle can be reached by taking a right turn in the centre of Ballylongford and following the signposts for the castle.

After departing Ballylongford, continue along the **R551**, passing through Asdee, before bearing right at the fork in the road 1km after the village. Although close to the coast, this stretch of road is quite hilly, with the local favourite, Beale Hill, thrown in as a warm-up to some of the more challenging climbs the Kerry section of the Wild Atlantic Way has to offer. Passing the spectacular Bromore Cliffs to the right, the route descends into the popular summer seaside resort of Ballybunion. This could be the place to grab an ice cream or a coffee before leaving town in southerly direction on Sandhill Road and cycling alongside the legendary golf course for a kilometre. The route pulls temporarily inland and back towards the **R551**, taking a right turn in the direction of Tralee.

Continue over the River Feale and up the hill to Ballyduff. On entering the village take the right-hand turn signposted for Causeway and Coast Road and proceed for 16km. It is along this open stretch of road to the northern side of Kerry Head that you get to see both what has gone and what is to come, with Ballybunion and Bromore in view to the north and the panorama of Kerry Head and the faint outline of the Dingle Peninsula over to the west.

Turn right at the unmarked T-junction and continue around Kerry Head in an anticlockwise direction. Here, parts of the route can be challenging and caution should be taken on certain parts of the road as it is quite broken; however, the views of Loop Head in Clare, Tralee Bay and the Dingle Peninsula make this section a visually memorable experience. The passage into Ballyheigue descends adjacent to the Atlantic, with the entrance to the village looming quite quickly ahead. Ballyheigue is a popular summer seaside village worth a few minutes of anyone's time, with a Blue Flag beach and enough cafés and shops to satisfy a quick refuel.

Once through the village take a right turn onto the **R551** in the direction of Tralee and Ardfert on a flat and open road, which gives distant views of the sand dunes over to the west and the flat agricultural farmlands of north Kerry to the east.

Wild Atlantic Way detour – Banna Strand

Between Ballyheigue and Ardfert lies the long, golden Banna Strand. Just a 4km return cycle from the main road, the beach was the landing point for Roger Casement and his two colleagues, who attempted to land a consignment of arms for the 1916 Easter uprising. A memorial stands close by. Nowadays the beach is a popular spot for walkers, water-sports enthusiasts and an annual Christmas Day swim.

A trail on Kerry Head with County Clare just visible in the background.

Milking time on Kerry Head.

On reaching the historical village of Ardfert, follow the one-way route around the village and past the medieval cathedral into the Square. Take the right turn signposted for Spa. Cycle past the large church and onto a narrow twisty road that is nicely sheltered by tall trees and hedgerows. Passing the turn for Tralee Golf Club, take the next right turn that leads off a slight ascent. Follow this winding road up through a couple of farmsteads that straddle either side of the road and proceed to the crossroads at Churchill. Follow the road in the direction of Fenit, enjoying a short but fast ascent that merges briefly with Barrow Harbour to the right. Take a right turn at the T-junction, just beyond the Old Lighthouse hotel, into Fenit village. In Fenit there are various options to refuel, with the convenience of a public toilet close to the beach.

On leaving Fenit the majority of the route to Tralee is accompanied by Tralee Bay on the right. The route passes quickly through Kilfenora and up the hill to The Spa. After leaving The Spa village continue to the next roundabout, adjacent to O'Donnell's pub in Tralee. Take the third exit and cycle down a steady house-lined road, the **R551**, towards the centre of Tralee. At the traffic lights take a right turn, following the Dingle signpost. Traverse the mini-roundabout and continue to the T-junction with the **N86**, close to Tralee Marina. Cycle alongside the canal in a westerly direction, passing through Blennerville village, identified by its distinctive white windmill. The final stretch of road for Day 1 runs fairly straight with some small hills to navigate before reaching Camp village. This area is dominated by Tralee Bay to the right and the Slieve Mish Mountains to the left. Continue straight through Camp, following the Conor Pass sign and cycling now on the **R560**. Within 8km, take the Castlegregory turning to the right, and enter the village. Well done: Day 1 is complete.

30. The Wild Atlantic Way – Day 2

Castlegregory – Dingle – Slea Head – Inch – Castlemaine – Killorglin – Glenbeigh

Day 2 starts with an early ascent of the Conor Pass, before fifty spellbinding kilometres around mystical Slea Head and then back along the west coastline until reaching mid-Kerry and the village of Glenbeigh.

Grade: 4/5

Height gain: 1,548m

Distance: 148km

Time: 6½ to 7½ hours

Climbs:

Category	Length	Start/End Points	Start/End Elevation	Average Gradient
2	5.1km	13.1km / 18.2km	54m / 478m	8.3%
5	4.3km	88.1km / 92.4km	4m / 122m	2.7%

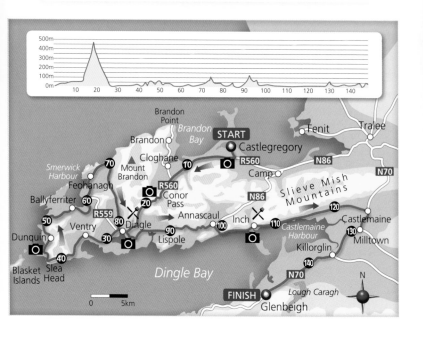

Looking back towards Slea Head from Ventry.

Start/Finish

Day 2 begins in Castlegregory and concludes in Glenbeigh.

Day 2 starts to deliver the Kerry as laid out by the mainstream guidebooks, with an early humdinger of a climb up the infamous Conor Pass, Ireland's highest mountain pass, followed swiftly by a 50km loop around the mystical and stunning Slea Head that is the filling between double visitations to Dingle town (although two visits to Dingle are still probably not enough). Once all of the ambience of west Kerry's main town has been absorbed there's the simple matter of following the yawning Castlemaine Harbour eastwards, passing the protracted yellow sands of Inch Strand and onto the Ring of Kerry route via Killorglin, renowned for the lively Puck Fair, with Day 2 concluding in Glenbeigh.

Route description

To begin Day 2 depart from Castlegregory southwards on the **R560**. On meeting the main Tralee-to-Conor Pass road turn right, following signposts for Dingle and the Conor Pass, cycling through the village of Stradbally before reaching the junction with Cloghane and Brandon Point.

Wild Atlantic Way detour – Brandon Point

At this point the Wild Atlantic Way branches off on an optional detour to Brandon Point. If time allows, this 27km round trip up to Brandon Point is well worth the trouble. The route, by and large, runs adjacent to small natural sea inlets, passing through the villages of Cloghane and Brandon, before rising up to Brandon Point. From here there are awesome views of the Dingle Peninsula, north Kerry and County Clare's Loop Head (weather permitting).

Once past the junction for Brandon Point the route moves inland towards the Conor Pass where the terrain alters from a seascape to an agricultural and forested expanse, interspersed by the occasional sheep farm, fresh mountain rivers and faraway mountain peaks.

The approach to the Conor Pass climb remains quite level, with the road signs and the Irish words *Go Mall* (Slow) painted on the road surface the giveaway that the climb is about to start. As the legs start adjusting to the ever-increasing gradient, the surrounding terrain is a mix of bare rock and woodland. Once at the halfway point of the climb, at Pedlar's Lake, the vista opens up to the right, with dazzling views of Clogharee Lough and Lough Gal shining mirrorlike amongst the green and yellow vegetation below.

Beyond Pedlar's Lake the climb alters slightly, insomuch as parts of the road are blasted into the side of the mountain, leaving small sections of the route very narrow in places and the mountainside within touching distance. Exercise caution in these areas as things can get tight. Once within striking distance of the summit the roadway opens up, though not before the mountain attempts one final sly kick, before the joy of a flat surface at the summit. Views at the top of the Conor Pass are not to be under appreciated, with both the view of the road already travelled back

Taking a breather above Coumeenoole Beach.

Quiet roads and ocean views on Slea Head, just before reaching Coumeenoole beach.

towards Castlegregory visible to the north-east and Dingle harbour in all its seaside glory visible to the south-west. Be aware that at the summit of the Conor Pass there can be poor visibility, strong winds and inclement weather.

With the Conor Pass ascent completed, the downward descent into Dingle is 7km long and a pleasurable experience. The surface of the road is excellent and the bends are gentle. On reaching Dingle take a left at the T-junction followed by a hasty right-hand turn, onto the **R559**. Continue to the next roundabout and take the second exit onto the Slea Head Drive, which is clearly signposted. Follow this route out of Dingle, with the marina to the left. At the roundabout beyond the Dingle Aquarium take the first exit signposted for Slea Head Drive, which will lead you onto the traditional clockwise direction for the Slea Head section. The first section of the route to Ventry is not too testing – in the main, rolling roads interspersed with mountain views – but as the road reaches Ventry, the Atlantic coastline opens up before you, revealing a sight that will make you want to explore more. Ventry is a picturesque village with a lovely beach that is just 5km from Dingle. Another 3km onwards is Ard a' Bhóthair, the village famous for being the home of the legendary Kerry footballer Páidí Ó Sé who has a statue to commemorate his life and many footballing achievements.

The next section of Slea Head is among the highlights of the Wild Atlantic Way in Kerry. For approximately the next 10km the road will slowly ascend and meander around the most westerly tip of the peninsula, with views of the ocean that make it hard not to stop at regular intervals to take it all in. There is a ford at one point that is easily crossed with a little due care, but otherwise the road, although narrow, is well enough surfaced for a comfortable journey. Keep along this road until you reach a signpost for Coumeenoole Beach. This beach, made famous by the film *Ryan's Daughter* in 1970, has dramatic views and is worth the slight detour down the ramp off the road to visit it.

Leaving Coumeenoole, continue for another 10km on through Dunquin and towards Ballyferriter. On this section the road widens significantly and from here on a clear day there are magnificent views of the Blasket Islands. Ballyferriter is a small village but very picturesque. It comes alive in the summer with many students taking advantage of the Irish-language courses held in various venues around the village.

Leaving Ballyferriter will mean that you are now turning east back towards Dingle and open views of the Atlantic begin to dramatically change as the landscape rises up from the sea before you towards Mount Brandon, which looms ahead in the distance. Not long after leaving Ballyferriter, take a left turn at the Smerwick Harbour Hotel, following signposts for Gallarus Oratory and Murreagh. Here the route passes by Gallarus Oratory, an early Christian church that should not be passed without a visit.

Leaving Gallarus, head north towards Murreagh and on along the coastline through Feohanagh. From here, the road rises over a distance of 3.5km and average gradient of 2.5%, leaving a little more than the stunning views and ancient architecture as a reminder of this stunning corner of Kerry. Once at the summit enjoy the remaining 6km into Dingle, which are mostly on a descent. In Dingle, the temptation for a coffee and a spot of lunch might prove too much. Indulge in some west Kerry hospitality at one of the fine eateries, with both traditional and artisanal menus on offer throughout the town.

Leaving Dingle, take the **N69** eastwards, following signposts for Tralee. The road out of town has a slight incline, but you are compensated with splendid views of Dingle Bay down to the right. Once past the Dingle racecourse, the road twists and turns before dropping down onto a long, straight section which carries on through into the village of Lispole, the birthplace of Thomas Ashe, a founding member of the Irish Volunteers and who died from being force-fed during a hunger strike whilst in incarceration in 1917. From here on there is a steady climb of 2.5km before a nice downhill stretch towards Annascaul that includes three hairpin bends. As the route enters Annascaul turn right onto the **R561** towards Inch and Castlemaine. This stretch of road follows the Annascaul River to its mouth at Bunaneer, before the road turns eastwards and embraces an exhilarating ocean ride that continues beyond Inch.

Inch Strand is always worth a stop, to view or even walk some of the 5km stretch of beach that gained renown after parts of the 1970s blockbuster film *Ryan's Daughter* were filmed in the location. The beach is now a very popular destination with surfers and walkers alike.

On the R561 between Annascaul and Inch, with Kells Bay ahead in the distance.

Continuing on the **R561**, the views are still excellent, with the Slieve Mish Mountains looming large to the left and clear views of Cromane, across Castlemaine Harbour, to the right. The road at this point is very straight and most of the route into Castlemaine consists now of small, rolling hills interspersed by flat sections.

On entering Castlemaine village take the right turn at the junction onto the **N70**, signposted for Killorglin. After crossing the bridge, turn right and continue into Milltown. Follow the road though the village and continue up the hill, heading westwards. Although the coastline has now disappeared from sight, it is never too far away, with Castlemaine Harbour just a few short kilometres over to the north-east. Within 7km of Milltown the route enters Killorglin, famous for Puck Fair, an event held annually every August and said to be one of Ireland's oldest fairs, dating back to 1603. Proceed over the River Laune Bridge and up the steep hill cutting through the centre of the town. At the mini-roundabout take the first exit and cycle westwards on the **N70** Ring of Kerry road towards Cahersiveen. From this point until Kenmare, 117km away, the Wild Atlantic Way and Ring of Kerry become the one route, bar a detour onto Valentia Island and the Skellig Ring.

With the ocean still out of sight, the route pushes on towards mountainous views of MacGillcuddy's Reeks to the south. The final stretch of today's itinerary between Killorglin and Glenbeigh is much flatter than what was encountered earlier in the day, but with just enough modest hills to remind you that there is still a small amount of work to be done before completing Day 2 into Glenbeigh.

31. The Wild Atlantic Way – Day 3

Glenbeigh – Cahersiveen – Valentia Island – Ballinskelligs – Waterville – Sneem – Kenmare – Ardgroom

A ferry journey, scenic islands and mountain passes add up to a show-stopping finale to this Wild Atlantic adventure.

Grade: 5			**Height gain:** 1,932m		
Distance: 161km			**Time:** 7 to 8 hours		
Climbs:					
Category	Length	Start/End Points	Start/End Elevation		Average Gradient
4	5.8km	2.2km / 8km	39m / 135m		1.6%
5	2.7km	32.13km / 34.83km	2m / 60m		2.1%
3	4.7km	40.23km / 44.94km	6m / 216m		4.5%
5	3.1km	49.44km / 52.54km	18m / 105m		2.8%
3	1.9km	70km / 71.9km	64m / 258m		10%
4	8.41km	89.37km / 97.78km	11m / 117m		1.3%
4	5.1km	144.32km / 149.42km	26m / 181m		3.0%

Start/Finish

Day 3 begins in Glenbeigh and concludes just over the county border in Ardgroom, County Cork, on the Beara Peninsula.

Day 3 of the Kerry Wild Atlantic Way route is certainly a test of endurance and climbing skills. This section of the route follows a large part of the famous Ring of Kerry on the Iveragh Peninsula, with the added bonus of Valentia Island, the Skellig Ring and the Kerry section of the Beara Peninsula. This final day of the route is a Wild Atlantic Way feast for the senses. This third day of the route is arguably the pinnacle of our three-day adventure. As the climbing becomes more frequent, a cyclist will be tempted to stop and enjoy the stunning views. The other dilemma about this part of the county is whether to explore the many detours on offer. Each justifies its own case for inclusion on the route for scenery, general beauty or historical value. Should anyone take the time to explore all these nooks and crannies, expect over 200km of an unforgettable final

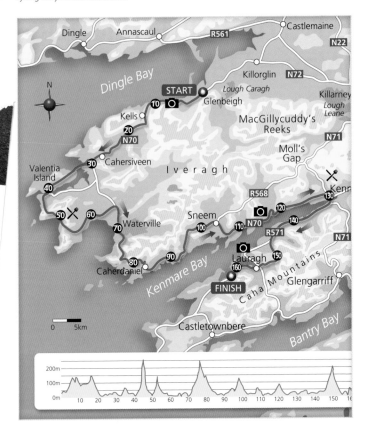

leg of Kerry's Wild Atlantic Way. Recommended detours on this route include but are not be limited to the following: Rossbeigh, Bealtra, Staigue Fort and Bunaw.

Route description

Departing westwards from Glenbeigh on the **N70** there is an early option to explore Rossbeigh.

Wild Atlantic Way detour – Rossbeigh

*Take a right turn at the end of Glenbeigh village onto the **R564**. The journey out to Rossbeigh is a 5km round trip, to an area of land dominated by sand dunes and beaches jutting northwards into Castlemaine Harbour. This area is popular with walkers and pony trekkers as well as hosting a horse race on the beach each year in late August.*

146

The beach at Rossbeigh.

Head off from Glenbeigh, following signposts for Cahersiveen. The climb out of Glenbeigh is steady before it levels out after 3 to 4km. The road sweeps along the coastline, revealing eye-catching vistas of the Dingle Peninsula and in particular Slea Head. For the next 6km the road hugs the undulating coast before climbing steadily in a south-westerly direction close to Kells Bay. The route then passes through a mountain-encompassed descent towards Cahersiveen. The road cuts straight through the heart of the town along the busy Main Street. Translated, Cahersiveen means 'Little Sadhbh's stone ringfort' referencing the many ringforts dotted around the area. At the southern end of the town, take the right turn for Reenard Point, signposted Skellig Ring via ferry. Note that the ferry is seasonal and operates every ten minutes from 7.45 a.m. to 9.30 p.m., seven days a week from 1 April to 31 October. The fee for a cyclist for the short ferry journey is approximately €2. In the event of the ferry not being in operation, the alternative route onto the island is to continue on the **N70**, taking a right turn onto the **R565** signposted for Portmagee. From the beginning of the **R565** the distance is 11 km to Portmagee and the bridge onto Valentia.

From the ferry, our route enters Knightstown, the largest village on Valentia Island. This was the base of operations for laying the transatlantic telegraph cable, which was completed in 1866. Pass through Knightstown and keep left, following signs for Portmagee. The 8km journey to Portmagee is slightly undulating, but it is hard to notice anything other than the views of the ocean and the mainland, as the road journeys through the quaint village of Chapeltown and on to the picturesque fishing village of Portmagee. The mainland and Portmagee are reached by crossing the Maurice O'Neill Bridge, which was built in 1970.

The ferry crossing to Valentia Island.

After crossing the bridge, turn right and travel through Portmagee, following signs for Ballinskelligs. Ahead lies Coomanaspic, a difficult category 3 climb that has an average gradient of 10% for close on 2km. On the summit, the views of Valentia Island behind and St Finian's Bay ahead are worth every vertical metre gained. Descend carefully through a number of switchbacks towards St Finian's Bay and you will be rewarded with breathtaking views ahead. Turn right at the base of the climb, passing Skelligs Chocolate Factory, a local industry that has an impressive array of unusual chocolate as well as a seating area, should you fancy a drink and a quick sample.

Follow the signposts for Ballinskelligs. Another climb awaits out of St Finian's Bay, this time less taxing than before, and eventually bringing you to the small Gaeltacht village of Ballinskelligs. From here, cycle 3km along the **R566**, crossing a bridge over the River Emlaghmore, prior to the junction with the **R567**. Turn right for Waterville and continue onto a T-junction with the **N70**. Take a right turn and travel to Waterville, less than 5km distant.

Waterville is famous for its connections with Charlie Chaplin and GAA footballer Mick O'Dwyer and is a very charming village, with its seafront promenade, beach and colourful buildings. Immediately after Waterville comes the ascent of Coomakista Pass. Although not an overly taxing climb, at 5.7km and a steady 3% it can be a challenging ascent on a blustery day. The scenery at the top of Coomakista is one of the main highlights of this section of the route, with stunning coastal views of O'Carroll's Cove and Derrynane to the fore and Waterville and Ballinskelligs Bay behind.

Travel onwards from the top of Coomakista and wind your way downwards on a well-surfaced road. Halfway down there is an opportunity to explore another branch of the route.

The view of O'Carroll's Cove between Waterville and Caherdaniel.

Wild Atlantic Way detour – Bealtra

Turn right just after the Scarriff Inn onto a road that twists and turns through a steep descent towards Bealtra Pier. This area is a popular walking trail, with the local Mass Path trail the highlight. The walk wends it way through to Derrynane on a scenic low-level coastal trail. The detour is 6km and is a straight out-and-back.

Quiet, well-surfaced roads on the way to Ballinskelligs.

Descending Coomakista.

Continuing on the main route, the road winds its way down to Caherdaniel and on towards Castlecove. Once past Castlecove, the road surface becomes somewhat lifeless – while being smooth and relatively flat, it is still hard work – in a 2km ascent to Crowley's Height, but the pacey descent towards Sneem comes as a welcome break with over 100km completed at this point. Sneem is a beautiful village that is divided in two by a river of the same name. It is a great base for visiting the many attractions nearby, such as Staigue Fort, an impressive ring fort said to date from the Iron Age.

After Sneem, continue along the main **N70** road, following signposts for Kenmare and passing the entrance to the renowned Parknasilla Hotel and Resort. Advance over the Blackwater Bridge and continue on alongside Kenmare Bay, which is by now well hidden by a mixture of woodland, shrubs and private properties, through Templenoe, before reaching Kenmare.

At the T-junction turn right and cycle into the centre of the town. Kenmare is translated from the Irish *Ceann Mara*, meaning 'head of the sea'. Although the modern town was laid out *c.* 1690, human occupation in the area has been traced back as far as 2200 to 500 BC. On leaving Kenmare travel southwards on the **N71** over Our Lady's Bridge across Kenmare Bay and take the next right-hand turn onto the **R571**, following signposts for Castletownbere. The early stages of the Beara Peninsula are on rolling roads that pass through woodland with sporadic views of Kenmare Bay to the right. Prior to the junction with Tousist the route commences a steady climb up alongside Knockanoughanish Mountain, which lies to the west. This area is certainly spectacular, a rugged green landscape dotted with countless mountaintops viewed in all directions. Once at the summit, the distant mountains loom over Kenmare Bay to the north, and the route travelled earlier appears to resemble little more than a track running alongside a distant lake.

The descent towards Lauragh is pleasant as the landscape turns from mountainous to lush, green terrain, interspersed by a few farms and local dwellings.

Wild Atlantic Way detour – Bunaw

As the route enters Lauragh there is an option to take a right turn onto the **R573** *towards Tousist and the Coast Road for a 7km out-and-back excursion, passing Derreen Gardens to the left before terminating at Bunaw, a pretty little coastal village and pier sitting inside a small natural harbour off Kenmare Bay.*

The final 8km on Kerry's Wild Atlantic Way are mainly sheltered on a tree-and-hedgerow-lined road, with sporadic views of Kenmare Bay to the north. The road rises and dips as it hugs the coastline for one last time before entering County Cork and a 3.5km cycle into Ardgroom village, reaching the end of your journey in a natural and wild setting that has scenery and tranquillity in abundance. Time now for quiet reflection on the road and journey just travelled, the highs and lows, the winds and the stillnesses, each pedal a metaphor for the daily grind in life but when a day ends as this one does, it is one to be cherished for a long time to come.

Signpost on the Wild Atlantic Way.